I0161526

RichThoughts
for Breakfast
Volume 8

Harold Herring

President of The Debt Free Army
& RichThoughts TV

www.HaroldHerring.com

Debt Free Army
PO Box 900000, Fort Worth, TX 76161

RichThoughts for Breakfast Volume 8
by Harold Herring

ISBN: 978-0-9763668-9-8
Copyright © 2019 by the Debt Free Army
PO Box 900000, Fort Worth, TX 76161
817-222-0011
harold@haroldherring.com

Unless otherwise noted, Scripture references are taken from the King James Version of the Bible.

RichThoughts for Breakfast
Volume 8
Table of Contents

7 M's to Your Success

I'm sure you probably eaten M&Ms (plain or my favorite with almonds) … No doubt you've used a variety of 3M products (sandpaper or Post-it notes) … but today I'm going to be sharing the 7 M's to your personal success.

1.   Mindset

Would you like to have the mindset of someone *who can overcome adversity … even the jealousy and lies of deceitful people* … turn defeat into victories … *create something out of nothing … turn economic failure into financial independence?* Of course you would.

Now here's the good news … *this mindset is available to you* … beginning right now … today.

First, get rid of the old way of thinking and doing.

Ezekiel 36:26-27 in the Contemporary English Version says:

> *"I will take away your stubborn heart and give*

you a new heart and a desire to be faithful. You will have only pure thoughts, because I will put my Spirit in you and make you eager to obey my laws and teachings."

Second, replace your old way of thinking with your new way of thinking.

Philippians 2:5 in the New Living Translation says:

"You must have the same attitude that Christ Jesus had."

Third, think on the pure, the powerful and the positive from the Word of God.

Philippians 4:8 in the Message Bible says:

"Summing it all up, friends, I'd say you'll do best by filling your minds and meditating on things true, noble, reputable, authentic, compelling, gracious—the best, not the worst; the beautiful, not the ugly; things to praise, not things to curse. Put into practice what you learned from me, what you heard and saw and realized."

Fourth, keep your mind focused on Him.

Philippians 4:7 says:

"And the peace of God, which passeth all understanding, shall keep your hearts and minds through Christ Jesus."

Fifth, use the mind of Christ that's within you ... allow it to function fully and freely.

1 Corinthians 2:16 in the Amplified Bible says:

"For who has known or understood the mind (the counsels and purposes) of the Lord so as to guide and instruct Him and give Him knowledge? But we have the mind of Christ (the Messiah) and do hold the thoughts (feelings and purposes) of His heart."

Sixth, allow the mind of Christ to direct your mindset on a daily basis.

Romans 12:2 in the New Living Translation says:

"... Let God transform you into a new person by changing the way you think."

Seventh, your mindset should always be to glorify God.

Romans 15:6 says:

"That ye may with one mind and one mouth glorify God, even the Father of our Lord Jesus Christ."

2. Motivation

Thousands, if not tens of thousands, of books have been written about motivation.

Here are 7 RichThoughts from the greatest motivational book ever written.

First, Ephesians 2:10 says:

"For we are <u>God's masterpiece</u>. He has created us anew in Christ Jesus, so we can do the good things he planned for us long ago."

Second, Psalm 37:4 says:

"Delight yourself in the Lord, and <u>He will give you the desires of your heart</u>."

Third, Psalm 37:23-24 says:

"<u>The Lord directs the steps of the godly</u>. He delights in every detail of their lives. Though they may stumble, they will never fall, for the Lord holds them by the hand."

Fourth, Ephesians 4:20 says:

"Now all glory to God, who is able, through <u>his mighty power at work within us, to accomplish infinitely more than we might ask or think</u>."

Fifth, Proverbs 3:5-6 says:

"<u>Trust in the Lord with all your heart</u>, and lean not on your own understanding; in all your ways acknowledge Him, and He shall direct your paths."

Sixth, Ephesians 6:7 says:

"Work with enthusiasm, as though you were working for the Lord rather than for people."

Seventh, Philippians 4:13 says:

"For I can do everything through Christ, who gives me strength."

In other words, you have unlimited opportunity and access.

Failure is not your destiny. Success is more than an option ... it is your God-given opportunity.

3.   Mobilization

The definition for mobilization according to diction-ary.com is:

"an act of assembling and putting into readiness for war or other emergency; organizing and making ready for use or action."

When you see or hear the word "war" no doubt you immediately think of a conflict between nations. How-ever, there is a war raging between believers and the enemy of our souls.

Make no doubt about it ... the enemy is relentless. He is continually bombarding our minds with negative and sinful thoughts … using diversionary tactics to break our focus.

The enemy knows *that if he can keep you from getting reinforcements (the Word) from headquarters (the church) he has a better chance of keeping you from speaking with your commanding officer (our great God Jehovah).*

4. Meticulous

Simply said, *pay attention to detail.*

Don't try to micro-manage every detail but *always in-spect what you expect to prevent defects in your plan.*

A meticulous person is accurate, exact, punctual, precise, attentive and careful.

I think it's fair to say that a *meticulous person is also a focused person.*

Focus can be simply defined as "whatever has your attention." It's clear that **God wants us focused on His plan for our lives.**

Don't let anyone's attitude or words distract you.

5. Marketable

The Bible provides us with excellent marketing strategies.

First, Hebrews 11:1 says:

"Now faith is the substance of things hoped for, the evidence of things not seen."

Your faith in God will loosen your creativity and ability to make something out of nothing. *That's what every start-up business leader must do.*

Second, Ecclesiastes 11:1 in the New Living Translation says:

"Send your grain across the seas, and in time, profits will flow back to you."

You may not see any immediate return … but always remember **that the progressive benefit is often much better than the immediate response.**

This scripture applies to investing in the stock market or commodities … you invest your time, effort and money … *knowing that you will receive a return* … because you've been guided by the Holy Spirit.

6.   Momentum

Momentum is best defined as:

"The amount of force a moving body has because of its weight and the speed at which it is moving."

Momentum works the same whether you're a short

person or a hefty one. If you take a big rock ... it will not travel very fast ... until you give it a push on a downhill slope ... then watch out.

The word momentum is not found in the scriptures ... however, I've identified two scriptures that speak to the heart this word.

Zechariah 4:10 tells us:

> *"Do not despise these small beginnings, for the LORD rejoices to see the work begin ..."*

It's not where you start in life ... it's where you end up. Your momentum (force) will either work for you or it won't.

That's why preparation time is important.

Zechariah 4:6 says:

> *"Not by might, nor by power, but by my spirit, saith the LORD of hosts."*

Every believer who uses principles based on the Word ... will be energized, enlightened and empowered by the Holy Spirit. **I can't think of a better way to create momentum for good than by obeying the voice of the Spirit.**

7.   Manifestation

Manifestation comes with expectation ... **whether**

in the marketplace, the secret place or your financial place.

Expectation brings manifestation and His rewards.

Proverbs 24:14 in the Amplified Bible says:

"So shall you know skillful and godly Wisdom to be thus to your life; if you find it, then shall there be a future and a reward, and your hope and expectation shall not be cut off."

No matter what your circumstances look like … *your expectation creates manifestation.*

The Message Bible translation of Proverbs 24:14 says:

"Likewise knowledge, and wisdom for your soul—Get that and your future's secured, your hope is on solid rock."

Child of God, are you getting this? **Your expectation secures your future, gives you a hope that is immoveable and a confidence in your impending manifestation.**

Your *future is secured when you expect to receive the manifestation of His best* … all God has to offer you.

One of the absolute worst things you could do while waiting for the manifestation of your harvest … is to stop sowing and just wait.

Day

2

7 Ways to Guarantee Your Financial Future

Your financial future is not based on the business or agency that writes your paycheck.

Nor is your financial future secured through your knowledge of the financial markets.

Neither is your financial future *safeguarded by the current contents of your retirement and/or investment portfolio.*

None of *the methods, knowledge or companies* I just mentioned can promise without fail ... your financial future.

However, there is *Someone who is ready, willing and able to direct your every step*.

Here are 7 ways to guarantee your financial future.

1. You must leave behind what's familiar when God tells you to do so.

Genesis 12:1 in the Amplified Bible says:

"NOW [in Haran] the Lord said to Abram, Go for yourself [for your own advantage] away from your country, from your relatives and your father's house, to the land that I will show you."

Leaving behind what's familiar to you ... *is not just family or a geographical location* **... it's also your old way of doing business.**

When you need money for a car ... repairs on that car ... tires ... groceries or anything else ... *if your first thought ... your first action is to whip out your credit card ... then you need to leave behind what's been familiar to you in the past.*

If you want God to secure your financial future ... you must trust Him to provide for every need you have.

More than ever before ... *we need to leave behind the world system of credit ... and move into a debt free lifestyle.*

2.   **Go where God tell you to go ... do what He tells you to do ... when He tells you to do it.**

Genesis 31:3 in the Amplified Bible says:

"And the LORD said unto Jacob, Return unto the land of thy fathers, and to thy kindred; and I will be with thee."

Sometimes when God tells us to do certain things ... *our natural minds resist because of what we perceive to be uncertain results* ... because *we cannot rationalize it by our normal way of thinking.*

Jacob had betrayed Esau ... had stolen his birthright. The scripture tells us he wasn't too anxious about seeing his brother again. In fact, Jacob was flat out afraid of what would happen when Esau saw him.

When Jacob came near to his brother ... he sent a message to Esau *advising him of the gifts he was bringing to him.*

The messenger returned to advise Jacob that Esau was on the way to meet him and he was traveling with four hundred men.

Frankly, this scared the bejeebers out of Jacob.

Genesis 32:7 says:

> *"Then Jacob was greatly afraid and distressed ..."*

When Esau arrived ... he greeted his brother with love. At first, he even *declined Jacob's generous gifts before reluctantly accepting them.*

However, the key verse is Genesis 33:11 in the New Living Translation which says:

> *"Please take this gift I have brought you, for God*

has been very gracious to me. I have more than enough." And because Jacob insisted, Esau finally accepted the gift."

Why was God gracious to Jacob … *because he went where He said to go … he did what God told him to do … so he was blessed and protected.*

3. The Lord's Prayer reveals that you're to never lack or fear over your finances.

Psalm 23:1 says:

"The Lord is my Shepherd; I shall not want."

According to *Strong's Concordance* the Hebrew word for *want* is chacer (H2637) and it means:

"to lack, be without, decrease, be lacking, have a need."

In fact, the Amplified Bible translation of Psalm 23:1 says:

"THE LORD is my Shepherd [to feed, guide, and shield me], I shall not lack."

God does not want you living in lack or needing a thing.

The Message Bible translation of Psalm 23:1 says:

"God, my shepherd! I don't need a thing."

Not only does He not want you living in lack ... he doesn't want you living in fear over lack.

4.   **Your attitude toward work ... will determine your future success ... and usefulness in the Kingdom.**

The New Living Translation of Proverbs 12:24 says:

"Work hard and become a leader; be lazy and become a slave."

God wants you to be a leader in the marketplace ... that's why you're here on planet earth. The earth is the Lord's, therefore it is *not unreasonable to understand that His children should be the ones dominating it.*

Ecclesiastes 3:22 in the New Living Translation says:

"So I saw that there is nothing better for people than to be happy in their work. That is why we are here! No one will bring us back from death to enjoy life after we die."

Not only are you to be a diligent worker ... but you need to be happy about it.

Ecclesiastes 2:24 in the New Living Translation says:

"So I decided there is nothing better than to enjoy food and drink and to find satisfaction in work. Then I realized that these pleasures are

from the hand of God."

5. Always remember … why you have what you have … and who gave it to you.

God brought you out of whatever mess you were in.

Deuteronomy 7:19 in the New Living Translation says:

"… And remember the miraculous signs and wonders, and the strong hand and powerful arm with which he brought you out of Egypt. The Lord your God will use this same power against all the people you fear."

Your most important financial relationship is not with your banker or broker but your Holy Ghost provider.

Luke 12:21 in the New Living Translation says:

"Yes, a person is a fool to store up earthly wealth but not have a rich relationship with God."

6. God secures your financial future by giving you an expert consultant.

If you have a lot of money … or, if you have any money … there is always someone willing to give you advice … even free advice.

Before buying into someone else's vision of your financial future … *chat with the consultant who will never have a conflict of interest.*

Over the years, I've had people offer me free advice on my financial affairs … but I knew *enough about sales techniques … to know when they were trying to steer the conversation … into a closing question for them.*

John 14:26 says:

"But the Comforter, which is the Holy Ghost, whom the Father will send in my name, he shall teach you all things, and bring all things to your remembrance, whatsoever I have said unto you."

Wow … I love this verse. **Hallelujah, He will bring ALL THINGS to my remembrance.**

7.   When you follow His instructions … God has plans for you.

Jeremiah 29:11 in the New International Version says:

"'For I know the plans I have for you,' declares the LORD, 'plans to prosper you and not to harm you, plans to give you hope and a future.'"

There are seven powerful thoughts in this verse.

- **First, He knows the plans He has for you.**

- **Second, God's plan is to prosper you.**

- **Third, God will never make plans that are harmful to you in any way.**

- **Fourth, God's plans are to give you hope.**

- **Fifth, God will give you a future.**

- **Sixth, God knows what He's doing when it comes to you.**

The Message Bible Translation of Jeremiah 29:11 says:

"I know what I'm doing. I have it all planned out—plans to take care of you, not abandon you, plans to give you the future you hope for."

- **Seventh, God will not only give you a future … He will give you the one you hoped for.**

Psalm 37:4 in the New Living Translation says:

"Take delight in the Lord, and he will give you your heart's desires."

Not only will God give you the future you hope for … the desires of your heart … He will ensure your personal success.

Psalm 20:4 in the New Living Translation says:

"May he grant your heart's desires and make all your plans succeed."

Now that's the kind of guarantee I like.

30 Success Principles from Proverbs

Day 3

Proverbs 22:17-20 in the Amplified Bible says:

"Listen (consent and submit) to the words of the wise, and apply your mind to my knowledge; for it will be pleasant if you keep them in your mind [believing them]; your lips will be accustomed to [confessing] them. So that your trust (belief, reliance, support, and confidence) may be in the Lord, I have made known these things to you today, even to you. Have I not written to you [long ago] excellent things in counsels and knowledge."

As I finished reading verse 20 … I felt impressed to read it in the New Living Translation which says:

"I have written thirty sayings for you, filled with advice and knowledge."

The phrase "thirty sayings" stirred my spirit so I read

verse 20 in the Message Bible which says:

"I'm giving you <u>thirty sterling principles</u>—tested guidelines to live by. Believe me—these are truths that work, and will keep you accountable to those who sent you."

After reading these various translations I was stirred to search the scriptures to find the 30 principles.

Imagine my joy when I found 30 sterling principles for success from Proverbs 22:17 to Proverbs 24:20.

Principle #1 – Be a listener and a learner.

Proverbs 22:17 in the Amplified Bible says:

"Listen (consent and submit) to the words of the wise, and apply your mind to my knowledge."

Principle #2 – Always be ready to speak of His peace, power, provision and protection.

Proverbs 22:18 in the Amplified Bible says:

"For it will be pleasant if you keep them in your mind [believing them]; your lips will be accustomed to [confessing] them."

Principle #3 – Learning is a daily discipline.

Proverbs 22:19 in the New Living Translation says:

"I am teaching you today—yes, you—so you will trust in the Lord."

Principle #4 – Always tell the truth.

Proverbs 22:21 says:

"That I might make thee know the certainty of the words of truth; that thou mightest answer the words of truth to them that send unto thee?"

Principle #5 – Don't take advantage of … cheat … or ignore the poor.

Proverbs 22:22 says:

"Rob not the poor, because he is poor: neither oppress the afflicted in the gate."

Principle #6 – Don't associate with angry, hot-tempered people.

Proverbs 22:24 says:

"Make no friendship with an angry man; and with a furious man thou shalt not go."

Principle #7 – Don't co-sign or guarantee someone else's debt.

Proverbs 22:26 in the Amplified Bible says:

"Be not one of those who strike hands and

pledge themselves, or of those who become se-curity for another's debts."

Proverbs 22:27 in the New Living Translation says:

"If you can't pay it [the debt], even your bed will be snatched from under you."

Principle #8 – Never claim as your own ... something that's clearly not.

Proverbs 22:28 in the New Living Translation says:

"Don't cheat your neighbor by moving the an-cient boundary markers set up by previous gen-erations."

Principle #9 – Excellence in the workplace will al-low you to work for important people.

Proverbs 22:29

"Seest thou a man diligent in his business? he shall stand before kings; he shall not stand be-fore mean men."

Principle #10 – Make good manners a lifestyle choice ... regardless of who you are eating with.

Proverbs 23:1-3 in the Message Bible says:

"When you go out to dinner with an influential person, mind your manners: Don't gobble your

food, don't talk with your mouth full. And don't stuff yourself; bridle your appetite."

Principle #11 – Don't chase money … let it chase you. When you do what's right money will be drawn to you.

Proverbs 23:4-5 says:

"Labour not to be rich: cease from thine own wisdom. Wilt thou set thine eyes upon that which is not? for riches certainly make themselves wings; they fly away as an eagle toward heaven."

As I was reading the Message Bible translation of Proverbs 23:4-5 … chasing the almighty dollar doesn't make you rich … but following His instructions does.

Principle #12 – Don't fellowship or even eat with stingy people.

Proverbs 23:6 says:

"Eat not the bread of him who has a hard, grudging, and envious eye, neither desire his dainty foods."

Principle #13 – Always make sure you're thinking about the right things for the right reasons.

Proverbs 23:7 says:

"For as he thinketh in his heart, so is he …"

Principle #14 – Never waste your time talking to fools … for they will never listen to or act on your words of wisdom.

Proverbs 23:9 says:

"Speak not in the ears of a fool: for he will despise the wisdom of thy words."

Principle #15 – You have a powerful Advocate to defend you against every attack of the enemy.

Proverbs 23:11 says:

"For their redeemer is mighty; he shall plead their cause with thee."

Principle #16 – Learning to understand what's important requires discipline on your part.

Proverbs 23:12 in the Amplified Bible says:

"Apply your mind to instruction and correction and your ears to words of knowledge."

Principle #17 – Failing to discipline a child now … will cause trouble later on.

Proverbs 23:13 says:

"Withhold not correction from the child: for if thou beatest him with the rod, he shall not die."

Principle #18 – The Word of God is always the right thing to speak … whether you're a child or an adult.

Proverbs 23:16 in the Amplified Bible says:

"Yes, my heart will rejoice when your lips speak right things."

Principle #19 – Never be jealous or envious of what sinners have but rather fear and honor the Lord … every moment of every day.

Proverbs 23:17 says:

"Let not thine heart envy sinners: but be thou in the fear of the LORD all the day long."

Principle #20 – When you do what's right in God's sight … you will always be rewarded and never disappointed.

Proverbs 23:18 in the Amplified Bible says:

"For surely there is a latter end [a future and a reward], and your hope and expectation shall not be cut off."

Principle #21 – Encourage your children, the people you supervise or mentor to always seek wisdom.

Proverbs 23:19 says:

"Hear thou, my son, and be wise, and guide

thine heart in the way."

Principle #22 – Avoid those who practice immorality or self-indulgence of any sort.

Proverbs 24:8-9 in the new Living Translation says:

"A person who plans evil will get a reputation as a troublemaker. The schemes of a fool are sinful; everyone detests a mocker."

Principle #23 – Listen to and honor your parents for their wisdom and insight.

Proverbs 23:24-25 in the New Living Translation says:

"The father of the [uncompromisingly] righteous (the upright, in right standing with God) shall greatly rejoice, and he who becomes the father of a wise child shall have joy in him. Let your father and your mother be glad, and let her who bore you rejoice."

Principle #24 – Live like God lives ... think as God thinks ... do what God does.

Proverbs 23:26 says:

"My son, give me thine heart, and let thine eyes observe my ways."

Principle #25 – Wisdom and understanding are the cornerstones of anything successful you build in

life … whether in the spiritual or the natural.

Proverbs 24:3-4 says:

"Through wisdom is an house builded; and by understanding it is established: And by knowledge shall the chambers be filled with all precious and pleasant riches."

Principle #26 – Create an inner circle of advisors known for their wisdom, strategic planning and good advice.

Proverbs 24:6 in the Amplified Bible says:

"For by wise counsel you can wage your war, and in an abundance of counselors there is victory and safety."

Principle #27 – Your response to adversity is a measure of your character.

Proverbs 24:10 in the Message Bible says:

"If you fall to pieces in a crisis, there wasn't much to you in the first place."

Principle #28 – Understand that God knows what you think and sees what you do … and you will be judged accordingly.

Proverbs 24:12 in the New Living Translation says:

"Don't excuse yourself by saying, `Look, we

didn't know.' For God understands all hearts, and he sees you. He who guards your soul knows you knew. He will repay all people as their actions deserve."

Principle #29 – If you mess up, fess up, get up and start again.

Proverbs 24:16 says:

"For a just man falleth seven times, and riseth up again: but the wicked shall fall into mischief."

Principle #30 – Take no pleasure in the failure of others.

Proverbs 24:19-20 in the New Living Translation says:

"Don't rejoice when your enemies fall; don't be happy when they stumble. For the Lord will be displeased with you and will turn his anger away from them."

And that's God's 30 sterling principles for success ... *as revealed in the book of Proverbs.*

Use them in your life ... and God will make you a success.

Day 4

7 Characteristics of the Kingly Anointing

Here are the seven characteristics of a kingly anointing.

1.   Honoring God as the Ultimate Authority of the Nation

Psalm 63:11 in the Amplified Bible says:

> *"But the king shall rejoice in God; everyone who swears by Him [that is, who binds himself by God's authority, acknowledging His supremacy, and devoting himself to His glory and service alone; every such one] shall glory, for the mouths of those who speak lies shall be stopped."*

The king is to be very vocal and visual in his recognition of God as the source of ultimate authority in the nation.

From the very beginning, most American presidents have recognized God as the ultimate authority in leading this nation.

President George Washington said:

"It is impossible to govern the world without God and the Bible."

One more quote from President Washington:

"Do not let anyone claim to be a true American if they ever attempt to remove religion from politics."

2.   Governing the Affairs of the People

Ecclesiastes 8:4 in the Amplified Bible says:

"For the word of a king is authority and power, and who can say to him, What are you doing?"

A wise king like Solomon desired the wisdom of God in governing the people more than anything else.

1 Kings 3:11-12 in the New Living Translation gives us God's response to King Solomon:

"So God replied, 'Because you have asked for wisdom in governing my people with justice and have not asked for a long life or wealth or the death of your enemies—I will give you what you asked for ...!'"

At times, the king would delegate his authority to someone he trusted to care for the people.

Genesis 41:39 in the New Living Translation says:

"So Pharaoh said to Joseph, 'You're the man for us. God has given you the inside story—no one is as qualified as you in experience and wisdom. From now on, you're in charge of my affairs; all my people will report to you. Only as king will I be over you.'"

Esther 10:3 in the New Living Translation says:

"Mordecai the Jew ranked second in command to King Xerxes. He was popular among the Jews and greatly respected by them. He worked hard for the good of his people; he cared for the peace and prosperity of his race."

It's interesting to me that both Pharaoh and King Xerxes put a Jew in as their second-in-command. Even heathen kings recognized the power of God working through His children.

3.   Protecting the Nation Against Attacks of Their Enemies

God wanted to be King over Israel but the people wanted a king they could see *even though his power was useless without God behind him.* But, from the very first king in Israel … it's clear the people wanted a king to protect them against their enemies.

1 Samuel 8:19 in the Message Bible says:

"But the people wouldn't listen to Samuel. 'No!'

they said. 'We will have a king to rule us! Then we'll be just like all the other nations. Our king will rule us and lead us and fight our battles.'"

4. Providing Tithes and Offerings to the Priests

2 Chronicles 24:11 in the New Living Translation says:

"Whenever the chest became full, the Levites would carry it to the king's officials. Then the court secretary and an officer of the high priest would come and empty the chest and take it back to the Temple again. This went on day after day, and a large amount of money was collected."

The king made sure there was provision through tithes and offerings for the priests and temple maintenance. The king too was expected to do his part.

5. Collecting the Spoils of War

The prize for every battle fought and won by the king and his men … were the spoils of war.

1 Chronicles 26:27 in the New King James Version says:

"Out of the spoils won in battles did they dedicate to maintain the house of the LORD."

One of my favorite passages is how God directed and

delivered not only a great victory to Jehoshaphat but the spoils of war as well.

2 Chronicles 20:25 in the New Living Translation says:

"King Jehoshaphat and his men went out to gather the plunder. They found vast amounts of equipment, clothing, and other valuables—more than they could carry. There was so much plunder that it took them three days just to collect it all!"

A king must always obey his ultimate authority ... *our great God Jehovah ... if he wants to be successful.*

6. Obeying the Instructions and Direction of God

The king is to set the standard for obedience in the kingdom. *People will always imitate the excellent of lifestyle and leadership provided by their king.*

2 Kings 23:25 in the New Living Translation says:

"Never before had there been a king like Josiah, who turned to the Lord with all his heart and soul and strength, obeying all the laws of Moses ..."

1 Kings 11:37 in the Message Bible says:

"But I have taken you in hand. Rule to your heart's content! You are to be the king of Israel. If you listen to what I tell you and live the way I

show you and do what pleases me, following directions and obeying orders as my servant David did, I'll stick with you no matter what. I'll build you a kingdom as solid as the one I built for David. Israel will be yours ..."

Whatever the king does set the tone for what the people will do.

7.   Settling Disputes Among His People

The one thing a king should want more than anything else is wisdom to rule his kingdom.

Notice the progression in 1 Kings 3:3-4 which says:

"And Solomon loved the LORD, walking in the statutes of David his father: only he sacrificed and burnt incense in high places ... a thousand burnt offerings did Solomon offer upon that altar."

First, the king brings an offering to God.

Next, 1 Kings 3:5 says:

"... the LORD appeared to Solomon in a dream by night: and God said, Ask what I shall give thee."

Second, God appeared to Solomon in a dream the night after he made his presentation of multiple offerings and asked him what He, God, could do for him.

In 1 Kings 3:9 in the Amplified Bible, it says:

"So give Your servant an understanding mind and a hearing heart to judge Your people, that I may discern between good and bad. For who is able to judge and rule this Your great people?"

Third, Solomon asks God for wisdom.

1 Kings 3:10 in the New Living Translation says:

"The Lord was pleased that Solomon had asked for wisdom."

Fourth, not only did King Solomon's offering please God … but his request for wisdom did as well.

Finally, 1 Kings 3:11-14 in the New Living Translation says:

"So God replied, 'Because you have asked for wisdom in governing my people with justice and have not asked for a long life or wealth or the death of your enemies—I will give you what you asked for! I will give you a wise and understanding heart such as no one else has had or ever will have! And I will also give you what you did not ask for—riches and fame! No other king in all the world will be compared to you for the rest of your life! And if you follow me and obey my decrees and my commands as your father, David, did, I will give you a long life.'"

By giving a proper offering ... by asking for wisdom ... King Solomon received riches, fame and a long life ... all by obeying and honoring God.

The test of the king's wisdom came in 1 Kings 3:16-27 when the two women living in the same house appeared before Solomon claiming to be the mother of one child. Using his God-given wisdom Solomon was able to discern right from wrong ... truth from a lie.

1 Kings 3:28 says:

> *"When all Israel heard the king's decision, the people were in awe of the king, for they saw the wisdom God had given him for rendering justice."*

In this teaching ... we can clearly see that a king and a priest are both known for their obedience to God's divine direction.

The great news is that the kingly and priestly anointing are both available to you today.

Day 5

God Wanted Me to Do This Again

Philippians 3:1 in the Amplified Bible says:

> *"FOR THE rest, my brethren, delight yourselves in the Lord and continue to rejoice that you are in Him. To keep writing to you [over and over] of the same things is not irksome to me, and it is [a precaution] for your safety."*

Last night, during our Sunday Night Live service … I taught a message titled, "7 Reasons Order Is Key to Your Success."

The text and email responses were such a blessing … even a couple of testimonies.

As I was meditating on the matter … I was given a very clear direction from the Lord to teach the seventh point specifically for you.

Faith cometh by hearing … and hearing … and hearing … and hearing … the Word of God.

Here are seven practical ideas on how to bring order

into your personal life.

First, bring order into your environment.

Remove clutter from your life including ... but not limited to ... *your desk*, dresser, *closet*, night stand, *bathroom reading rack*, medicine cabinet, *garage*, attic and ... well, *everything else* ... including your closets.

Smiling. I love you and God loves you.

We were in the process of selling our home several years ago ... *my wife had done an excellent job in "Feng Shui-ing" the house ... which means removing the clutter and simplifying the look ... thus allowing potential buyers to see themselves living there.* She, however, calls it *Holy Ghost "shui-ing" it because the Holy Spirit helped her make the decisions.*

Ask God how to bring order into your environment ... *He will gladly reveal it to you.*

Psalm 32:8 in the English Standard Version (ESV) says:

> *"I will instruct you and teach you in the way you should go; I will counsel you with my eye upon you."*

Second, bring order into your job, business or retirement.

Let's start with your car ... *the interior and exterior of your car reflect the order in your life.* If there's stuff in the floorboard ... *it sends a message ... and not the one you necessarily want. Clean it up ... and keep it tidy every day.*

Your office desk, workstation and files are a reflection of whether or not your professional life is in order. I almost forgot ... your briefcase.

Whether or not you are late for appointments or meetings is another indicator of whether or not ... you'll be in line for promotion.

If you're retired ... *is there an order to your day* ... do you have a plan for your week?

1 Timothy 4:15 in the New Living Translation says:

> *"Give your complete attention to these matters. Throw yourself into your tasks so that everyone will see your progress."*

Third, bring order into your spiritual, mental and physical thought-processes and actions.

The best way to bring order to your thought-processes is three-fold.

First, in Romans 12:2 in the New Living Translation it says:

> *"Let God transform you into a new person by changing the way you think."*

Second, Philippians 2:2 in the Amplified Bible says:

"Fill up and complete my joy by living in harmony and being of the same mind and one in purpose, having the same love, being in full accord and of one harmonious mind and intention."

Third, visit www.HaroldHerring.com and read "7 Things to Do Before You Go to Sleep" over and over again … until it becomes as routine as breathing.

- *First*, create a to-do list of the things you plan to accomplish tomorrow.

- *Second*, journal the great things that happened to you during the day.

- *Third*, create a nightly confession about tomorrow being the best day of your life.

- *Fourth*, never go to bed mad or frustrated with your spouse or children.

- *Fifth*, clean up … pick up … so you'll be ready to get up.

- *Sixth*, lay out what you plan to wear tomorrow.

- *Seventh*, plan how you will dress your mind tomorrow.

Fourth, bring order into your choice of friends and their rotation in and out of your circle of influence.

This is really simple.

If your friends aren't motivated toward success or seeking a better quality of life for themselves and their families ... *then a large part of your life will naturally be in disorder.*

I'm not telling you to dump the old friends ... but I'm definitely recommending you get some new ones ... *whose motivation, beliefs and lifestyle promote order.*

1 Corinthians 15:33 in the Amplified Bible says:

> *"Do not be so deceived and misled! Evil companionships (communion, associations) corrupt and deprave good manners and morals and character."*

Fifth, bring order into your habits.

Strengthen habits that bring order into your life and release those that don't.

Don't ask me why ... *but several things immediately came to mind when I started typing this point.*

- Make sure you get a proper amount of exercise.

- Stay hydrated ... *drink half of your body weight in ounces of water* ... which will increase your energy level and removes toxins.

- Change your toothbrush every 90 days ... *removing the possibility of bacteria from your life.* (This should become a routine procedure.)

- Finally, organize your photos ... perhaps even scanning them into your computer.

Literally, there are dozens and dozens of other things I could have written but these are the ones that came to mind.

Job 22:26 in the Amplified Bible says:

"You shall also decide and decree a thing, and it shall be established for you; and the light [of God's favor] shall shine upon your ways."

Sixth, bring order into your daily routines.

Do you know what CDs you'll be listening to as you drive to work ... or take the kids to school and run errands?

Do you have a regularly scheduled time to read ... and I'm not just talking about your morning devotional. Books that fire you up ... make you think beyond your imagination.

Bring order into the ways you shop. *Always go with a list.*

Give careful thought to the days you shop. *For instance, never go to Walmart on Saturday unless you go early in the morning.* The same is true with visits to the grocery store.

If you're married … always … have quality time with your spouse. *Make every activity a date* … in addition to regular date nights.

The key to maintaining order in your daily life … is to stay fresh. *Schedule time to reflect and re-direct your focus.*

Lamentations 3:40 in the New Living Translation says:

> *"Instead, let us test and examine our ways. Let us turn back to the Lord."*

Seventh, bring order into your finances.

The best way to bring order into your financial arena is with a plan to get out of debt or a plan to never get in debt again.

Never make a major purchase without talking to God (and your spouse, if married) about it.

If you're serious about getting out of debt … I will email you a download of The Master Plan, our interactive personalized out-of-debt plan. When you complete the plan … you will know the exact day, month and year you will be completely debt free. This life-changing tool normally sells for $50 but I'll send it to you as a seed. Just send an email to Harold@harold herring.com. If you don't do email … send me a letter requesting The Master Plan and I'll send you a CD.

If you want more information on financial order ... visit www.HaroldHerring.com and read my various blogs on the subject.

Luke 14:28-30 in the Message Bible says:

"Is there anyone here who, planning to build a new house, doesn't first sit down and figure the cost so you'll know if you can complete it? If you only get the foundation laid and then run out of money, you're going to look pretty foolish. Everyone passing by will poke fun at you: 'He started something he couldn't finish.'"

Two final scriptures ...

Proverbs 12:27 in the Message Bible says:

"A lazy life is an empty life, but 'early to rise' gets the job done."

When you bring order into your life ... then you will find extra satisfaction as seen in Deuteronomy 12:16 in the Message Bible:

"... You are to celebrate in the Presence of God, your God, all the things you've been able to accomplish."

Day 6

7 Reasons You Need a Good Reputation

Are you known as someone who keeps their word?

Are you recognized as someone whose opinion has value?

Are you thought of as someone who pays their debts *or someone who never does?*

Are you viewed as a positive and enthusiastic person that people enjoy being around or … *are you some-one who is avoided because of the words that come out of your mouth?*

Are you valued as the kind of friend who will stick with someone … through thick and thin?

Are you well-known *as a Christian … because of the words you speak and the life you live?*

What kind of reputation did you have … in high school and college?

I remember being told to avoid certain people ... especially girls because they had a bad reputation.

Sadly ... sometimes correctly and at times incorrectly ... girls more so than boys were characterized by their perceived or actual promiscuity.

Times have changed ... as witnessed by journalist and author, Linda Chavez.

"Back in the day, a pair of tight jeans was enough to earn a girl a bad reputation. Now slutty has gone Main Street."

Enough said.

Have you ever commented personally on someone's reputation ... *or the lack of it?*

Your reputation goes before you ... it can either open or close doors for you.

Have you ever told someone or been told that ... *"your reputation precedes you"* ?

Your reputation will go places you've never been or before people you've never met.

You will be profiled by your reputation of the past ... until you do something to change your reputation of the future.

Here are seven reasons you need a good reputation.

1.   A good reputation will give you power.

Esther 9:4 in the New International Version says:

"Mordecai was prominent in the palace; his reputation spread throughout the provinces, and he became more and more powerful."

With power comes the ability to create success … *where that possibility didn't previously exist.*

Euripides said:

> **"Along with success comes a reputation for wisdom."**

A good reputation brings wisdom, power and success. It should also be noted that Publilius Syrus, the first century orator, said:

> **"A good reputation is more valuable than money."**

2.   A good reputation will help you avoid traps of the enemy.

People who are concerned about their reputation or have spent their lives building a good one … *will think twice before yielding to temptation or falling prey to tricks of the enemy.*

1 Timothy 3:7 in the New International Version says:

"He must also have a good reputation with out-siders, so that he will not fall into disgrace and into the devil's trap."

3.   A good reputation comes from service to others.

Jim Rohn, the great author and motivational speaker, said:

"Whoever renders service to many *puts him-self in line for greatness - great wealth*, great return, *great satisfaction*, great reputation, and *great joy*."

1 Timothy 5:10 in the Amplified Bible says:

"And she must have a reputation for good deeds, as one who has brought up children, who has practiced hospitality to strangers [of the brotherhood], washed the feet of the saints, helped to relieve the distressed, [and] devoted herself diligently to doing good in every way."

Are you known as a servant to others … is that part of your reputation?

4.   A leader without a good reputation is head-ed for trouble.

1 Chronicles 5:24-26 in The Living Bible says:

"Each of these men had a great reputation as a warrior and leader. But they were not true to the God of their fathers; instead they worshiped the idols of the people whom God had destroyed. So God caused King Pul of Assyria (also known as Tilgath-pilneser III) to invade the land and deport the men of Reuben, Gad, and the half-tribe of Manasseh. They took them to Halah, Habor, Hara, and the Gozan River, where they remain to this day."

Your reputation is often assumed or determined by the people you associate with.

President George Washington said:

"Associate with men of good quality if you esteem your own reputation; for it is better to be alone than in bad company."

5.   The actions of a person with a good reputation will never be forgotten.

Nehemiah 9:10-11 in The Living Bible says:

"You displayed great miracles against Pharaoh and his people, for you knew how brutally the Egyptians were treating them; you have a glorious reputation because of those never-to-be-forgotten deeds."

By the same token … *a reputation that you've taken years to build can be destroyed in a matter of days.*

Consider how you now view former Governor Arnold Schwarzenegger or former Congressman Anthony Weiner.

Warren Buffett, one of the wealthiest men in the world, said:

"It takes 20 years to build a reputation and five minutes to ruin it. If you think about that, you'll do things differently."

I also want to share a quote by Joseph Hall, an American clergyman from the 16th century, who said:

"A reputation once broken may possibly be repaired, but the world will always keep their eyes on the spot where the crack was."

6.   People with a good reputation are celebrated.

Psalm 89:16-18 in The Living Bible says:

"They rejoice all day long in your wonderful reputation and in your perfect righteousness. You are their strength. What glory! Our power is based on your favor!"

A person with a good reputation ... is most often a person of character.

John Wooden, the great basketball coach, said:

"Be more concerned with your character than your reputation, because your character is what you really are, while your reputation is merely what others think you are."

Benjamin Franklin, the American statesman said:

"It takes many good deeds to build a good reputation, and only one bad one to lose it."

7.   A person with a good reputation is highly valued.

Ecclesiastes 7:1 in The Living Bible says:

"A good reputation is more valuable than the most expensive perfume."

Proverbs 3:4-6 in The Living Bible says:

"If you want favor with both God and man, and a reputation for good judgment and common sense, then trust the Lord completely; don't ever trust yourself. In everything you do, put God first, and he will direct you and crown your efforts with success."

Reputations are built on action, inaction and reaction.

Henry Ford said:

"You can't build a reputation on what you are going to do."

Remember, reputations are built every moment of every day ... by everything you do or fail to do.

Finally, here are sixteen ways to build and maintain a good reputation ... and they're all found in Philippians 4:8 in the Amplified Bible which says:

> *"For the rest, brethren, whatever is <u>true</u>, whatever is <u>worthy of reverence</u> and is <u>honorable</u> and <u>seemly</u>, whatever is <u>just</u>, whatever is <u>pure</u>, whatever is <u>lovely and lovable</u>, whatever is <u>kind</u> and <u>winsome</u> and <u>gracious</u>, if there is any <u>virtue</u> and <u>excellence</u>, if there is anything <u>worthy of praise</u>, <u>think on</u> and <u>weigh and take account of these things</u> [<u>**fix your minds on them**</u>]."*

Think about it ... then do it.

Day 7

I Will Bless You with Everything I Have

Caution: The scriptures I'm about to share with you … *may cause a Holy Ghost explosion in your spirit. You might find yourself shouting* … maybe even running around the room … *but one thing is for sure … you will be PRAISING GOD.*

Hebrews 6:14 says:

> *"Saying, Surely blessing I will bless thee, and multiplying I will multiply thee."*

As I was reading this scripture … it ignited in my spirit … I decided to read it in several other translations.

Hebrews 6:14 in the Message Bible says:

> *"He said, 'I promise that I'll bless you with every-thing I have—bless and bless and bless!'"*

Personalize this scripture … LeJune, Raymond, Ja-nine, Michelle …

"He said, 'I promise that I'll bless <<Your Name>> with everything I have—bless and bless and bless!'"

Wow … God says, **"I will bless you with everything I have."** That sounds amazing! Are we taking God up on that promise … today?

Sadly, there are *some people who love God with all their hearts but "they think" when the scripture says God will bless us* … it refers only to eternal life … *the sweet by and by.*

But that's *just not* what the scripture means.

For instance, according to *Strong's Concordance,* the word bless found in Hebrews 6:14 is the Greek word (yeah la gay o) eulogeo and it means, among other things:

**"to cause to prosper; to make happy;
to be favored of God."**

We're talking about being blessed, prospered and favored of God … *right here … right now.*

It's not God's desire for you to be broke and in debt up to your eyebrows.

God wants you prosperous … **He wants you blessed to be a blessing to others.**

You can't bless someone else *if you're broke, unhap-*

py, playing the blame game, walking in guilt and relying on excuses as to why you're not where you know you ought to be.

It's not God's desire for you to always look like you were weaned on a dill pickle. God wants you happy … *but more than that* … He wants you full of His joy.

Happiness is external and relies on your circumstances … being broke is certainly not a happy circumstance.

Whereas, *joy is internal* and is *based on your knowledge of the Word and your understanding that no matter what happens around you* … **God will always direct your path to His desired blessing flow for your life**.

*The word **bless** also means you're to be favored of God.*

When I was directed to Galatians 3:9 in the Amplified Bible I smiled … big time. The verse says:

> *"So then, those who are people of faith are blessed and made happy and favored by God [as partners in fellowship] with the believing and trusting Abraham."*

The word *blessed* in this verse is the same Greek word used in Hebrews 6:14.

As you remember, it's the Greek word (ya la gay o)

eulogeō (G2127) which means among other things:

**"to cause to prosper; to make happy;
to be favored of God."**

Now let's look at Galatians 3:9 again … this time in the Contemporary English Version which says:

"This means that everyone who has faith will share in the blessings that were given to Abraham because of his faith."

Personalize this with your name … Pat, Derek, Jean Marie, Asako …

"This means that <<Your Name>> who has faith will share in the blessings that were given to Abraham because of his faith."

Seems like a good time to look at Genesis 22:15 in the Message Bible:

"The angel of God spoke from Heaven a second time to Abraham: 'I swear—God's sure word!— because you have gone through with this, and have not refused to give me your son, your dear, dear son, I'll bless you—oh, how I'll bless you! And I'll make sure that your children flourish— like stars in the sky! like sand on the beaches! And your descendants will defeat their enemies. All nations on Earth will find themselves blessed through your descendants because you obeyed me.'"

It's clear to me … we're blessed because we're the descendants of Abraham.

Acts 3:25 in the Amplified Bible says:

"You are the descendants (sons) of the prophets and the heirs of the covenant which God made and gave to your forefathers, saying to Abraham, And in your Seed (Heir) shall all the families of the earth be blessed and benefited."

Just as God promised to bless Abraham, He will also bless us.

Why does God desire to bless His people? So we might establish His covenant … we are blessed to be a blessing to others (Deuteronomy 8:18).

All the promises and blessings of Abraham belong to you and me according to Genesis 22:18:

"And in thy seed shall all the nations of the earth be blessed; because thou hast obeyed my voice."

Let's look at Acts 3:25 in the Amplified Bible again … where it says:

"You are the descendants (sons) of the prophets and the heirs of the covenant which God made and gave to your forefathers, saying to Abraham, And in your Seed (Heir) shall all the families of the earth be blessed and benefited."

Are you ready for this?

You are blessed or will be blessed so that you can be a blessing to others.

God does not prosper you for the purpose of raising your standard of living. <u>He prospers you so that you can raise your standard of giving</u>.

The call of God upon Abraham can be the model for God's call to us.

Just as God promised to bless Abraham, He also will bless us. Why does God desire to bless His people? So that we might establish His covenant ... we are blessed to be a blessing to others.

2 Corinthians 9:8 in the Amplified Bible says:

> *"And God is able to make all grace (every favor and earthly blessing) come to you in abundance, so that you may always and under all circumstances and whatever the need be self-sufficient [possessing enough to require no aid or support and furnished in abundance for every good work and charitable donation]."*

We're also blessed because we praise Him.

Psalm 145:2 in the Amplified Bible says:

> *"Every day [with its new reasons] will I bless You [affectionately and gratefully praise You]; yes, I*

will praise Your name forever and ever."

As we praise Him … He blesses us … as we walk in His righteousness … He blesses us.

Proverbs 3:33 in the Amplified Bible says:

> *"The curse of the Lord is in and on the house of the wicked, <u>but He declares blessed</u> <u>(joyful and favored with blessings</u>) the home of the just and consistently righteous."*

When we do what's right before Him … when we obey His instructions … He will bless us beyond measure.

Ephesians 1:3 in the Amplified Bible says:

> *"May blessing (praise, laudation, and eulogy) be to the God and Father of our Lord Jesus Christ (the Messiah) Who has blessed us in Christ with every spiritual (given by the Holy Spirit) blessing in the heavenly realm!"*

I like that … **He is going to give us every blessing from the heavenly realm.**

The last scripture I was led to was Jeremiah 32:40 in the New Living Translation which says:

> *"And I will make an everlasting covenant with them: I will never stop doing good for them. I will put a desire in their hearts to worship me, and they will never leave me."*

Personalize this scripture … Kim, Justin, Shelia …

"And I will make an everlasting covenant with <<Your Name>>: I will never stop doing good for <<Your Name>>. I will put a desire in <<Your Name>>'s heart to worship me, and <<he/she>> will never leave me."

Not only is God going to cause us to prosper; to make us happy and to walk in His favor … **He is never going to stop doing good for us** … and He will never leave us.

Now that's what I call a blessing flow.

Day 8

God Chose You for Something Special

When you were a kid … *did you ever play any games where two leaders took turns* and picked to determine whose side you would play on?

As a boy, we chose sides while playing all sporting events. If you were athletically challenged … you were the last kid who was "grudgingly" chosen.

I remember the last player being chosen with an air of disgust … *since the team would be "stuck" with the least athletic player*.

Fortunately for my self-esteem, I was never the last player to be chosen … *but I can empathize with how the last kid picked must have felt.*

I've got a revelation for you … **when it comes to God's team … you are always first**.

Even if all the rest of the people born on planet earth were accounted for … *and you turned up lost … the Shepherd of your soul would search after you*.

Luke 15:4 in the New Living Translation says:

"If a man has a hundred sheep and one of them gets lost, what will he do? Won't he leave the ninety-nine others in the wilderness and go to search for the one that is lost until he finds it?"

1 Thessalonians 4:4 in the Amplified Bible says:

"[O] brethren beloved by God, we recognize and know that He has selected (chosen) you,"

Are you hearing this? Of all the people who are currently drawing a breath on planet earth ... God, the Master of the Universe ... *has chosen you.*

The Message Bible translation of 1 Thessalonians 4:4-5 says:

"... God not only loves you very much but also has put his hand on you for something special. When the Message we preached came to you, it wasn't just words. Something happened in you. The Holy Spirit put steel in your convictions."

Personalize this verse ... Colette ... Katherine ... Paul ...

"... God not only loves <<Your Name>> very much but also has put his hand on <<him/her>> for something special. When the Message we preached came to <<Your Name>>, it wasn't just words. Something happened in <<Your

Name>>. The Holy Spirit put steel in <<his/her>> convictions."

It doesn't matter whether you can play sports, *an instrument in the band* or sing in the Glee Club … *you have something special to achieve in your life because God made sure you were born.*

Here are five things to know about your special assignment.

1.   God loves you very much.

I remember the song I sang as a kid in Sunday School and truthfully still do.

"Jesus loves me this I know for the Bible tells me so …"

How can we be so sure that God loves us so very much? It's simple, *He sent His very best* and I'm not talking about a Hallmark card.

John 3:16 says:

"For God so loved the world, that he gave his only begotten Son, that whosoever believeth in him should not perish, but have everlasting life."

You know God must love you … *because He allowed His only Son to be wrongly accused, tried, persecuted, tortured and killed* FOR YOU. God did all of that because He loves you so very much.

John 16:27 in the Contemporary English Version says:

"God the Father loves you because you love me, and you believe that I have come from him."

2. God has His hand on you for a special assignment.

The scripture in 1 Thessalonians 4:4 is clear … God has something special for you to do with your life.

Jeremiah 29:11 in the New International Version says:

"'For I know the plans I have for you,' declares the LORD, 'plans to prosper you and not to harm you, plans to give you hope and a future.'"

However, *you must be willing to accept and act on His plans for your life.*

Numbers 30:2 in the New Century Version says:

"If a man makes a promise to the Lord or says he will do something special, he must keep his promise. He must do what he said."

God's assignment for your life isn't something that just happens … *once revealed … you seek His direction and write out your plans to accomplish that something special.*

2 Timothy 1:1 in the Message Bible says:

"I, Paul, am on special assignment for Christ, carrying out God's plan laid out in the Message of Life by Jesus. I write this to you, Timothy, the son I love so much. All the best from our God and Christ be yours! To Be Bold with God's Gifts.]"

3. God's Words should never flow in one ear and out the other.

If something goes in one ear and out the other … it means that you either *(a) weren't focused on what was being said; (b) didn't understand or comprehend what was said; (c) were bored by what was said.*

I strongly recommend you don't daydream when the Word of God is spoken.

Matthew 13:13 in the Message Bible says:

"This is the reason that I speak to them in parables: because having the power of seeing, they do not see; and having the power of hearing, they do not hear, nor do they grasp and understand."

When you hear, receive and understand His words … you will be blessed even more.

Mark 4:24 in the New Living Translation says:

"Then he added, 'Pay close attention to what you hear. The closer you listen, the more under-

*standing you will be given —and you will receive
even more.'"*

4.   God's Word will change you.

The Word of God can soften the hardest heart ...
*wash away the darkest sin ... tame the most rebel-
lious heart ... turn the worst sinner into the best saint*
and yes, *it can give you life ... abundantly (now) and
eternally.*

John 6:63 in the Amplified Bible says:

> *"It is the Spirit Who gives life [He is the Life-
> giver]; the flesh conveys no benefit whatever
> [there is no profit in it]. The words (truths) that I
> have been speaking to you are spirit and life."*

Luke 13:3 in the Amplified Bible says:

> *"I tell you, No; but unless you repent (change
> your mind for the better and heartily amend your
> ways, with abhorrence of your past sins), you
> will all likewise perish and be lost eternally."*

Proverbs 18:20 in the Contemporary English Version
says:

> *"Make your words good— you will be glad you
> did."*

5.   The Holy Spirit will give you a backbone.

Were you ever picked on by bullies at school? *Was there ever a time where an older sibling or someone else came to your rescue?* How did it make you feel? Invincible?

Isn't it nice to know that your older brother, *Jesus, is always ready to make the bully of this world tuck his tail and run for the door?*

Joshua 10:8 in the New Living Translation says:

"'Do not be afraid of them,' the Lord said to Joshua, 'for I have given you victory over them. Not a single one of them will be able to stand up to you.'"

You will never have to face any battle alone.

Mark 9:27 in the New Century Version says:

"Jesus took his hand and helped him to stand up."

Hebrews 13:5 in the Amplified Bible says:

"Let your character or moral disposition be free from love of money [including greed, avarice, lust, and craving for earthly possessions] and be satisfied with your present [circumstances and with what you have]; for He [God] Himself has said, I will not in any way fail you nor give you up nor leave you without support. [I will] not,[I will] not, [I will] not in any degree leave you helpless

nor forsake nor let [you] down (relax My hold on you)! [Assuredly not!]"

One final note, God chose you first ... because He's got something special for you to do ... it's time that you stand up to the occasion.

Day 9

7 Reasons to Do Your Best

I felt promoted to look up "best" at dictionary.com where it is defined as:

"Of the highest quality, excellence, or standing; something or someone that is best."

Without question, our Heavenly Father, **in His compassion for us ...** *gave someone of the "highest quality, excellence and standing" ...* **He gave** *His* **best ...** *His only begotten Son so that* ***you and I might have life and might have it more abundantly*** (John 10:10).

Since God gave His best for us ... **should we give any less to Him?**

Do we give God **our best moments in prayer and meditation on His Word or do we give Him the residue ... the remains of our day**?

Do we give our best effort on the *job or do we do **just enough to get by** and **receive a paycheck**?*

Do we give our **best offerings to God or just tip Him**?

As I was thinking about this, I was **led very specifically to Proverbs 3:9**:

"Honour the LORD with thy substance, and with the firstfruits of all thine increase."

The New Living Translation says:

"Honor the Lord with your wealth and with the best part of everything you produce."

The Message Bible says:

"Honor God with everything you own; give him the first and the best."

The scripture says that **we HONOR the Lord ... when we give Him our best**.

The firstfruits represent the best part of everything we produce.

When we finally realize that everything we own belongs to Him, it makes our giving much easier and certainly more joyful. We don't own it anyway.

If He wants to use some of it for the Kingdom, *He has every right to do so*.

However, **God doesn't want all you have ... He just**

wants your best.

What is your best offering? Truthfully *... that's determined every time He tells you to give.*

Your best in one offering may not be your best in the next. *That's why we should seek His direction every time there is an offering and listen to what He says.* **Determine what He would have you give as your best seed** *at that moment.*

It's also important to understand that **the best offering is not a set amount** ... *it's whatever He says, whenever He says it and to whomever He tells us to give.*

In reading these two scriptures, it's very clear that **God wants our best gifts. <u>He does not want to be tipped</u>** ... *<u>He does not want to be patronized with less than the best</u>.*

Every time you're in a service ... whether it's a **church service** or a ministry meeting like the seminars I hold for the Debt Free Army ... during the offering ... **do you ask yourself what is the very best gift that God would have you give**?

Now let me ask you another question.

If we HONOR THE LORD with our wealth <u>and the best that we produce as the scripture says</u> ... *doesn't it stand to reason that we dishonor Him when we give less than the best*?

At offering time ... **we honor God by obeying His commands**. That is giving Him our best.

The dictionary defines honor as:

> **"high respect, as for worth, merit, or rank."**

So it <u>**stands to reason that if we don't give God the first**</u>, *the best of everything we have*, **then we are not giving Him the highest respect**.

Numbers 18:29 in the New Living Translation says:

> *"Be sure to give to the Lord the best portions of the gifts given to you."*

What are the gifts given to you?

Is time a gift? *Do you give Him the best part of your day ... when you're refreshed, relaxed and ready to enter into His presence?*

It's clear to me ... that **God wants our best ...** *not excuses ...* **not promises of what we'll do one day ... when it's convenient.** *He's wants our best now* <u>**and that's how we honor Him every day we live**</u>.

The words of Colossians 1:28-29 in the Message Bible are a good way to encapsulate this message.

> *"We teach in a spirit of profound common sense so that we can bring each person to maturity. To*

be mature is to be basic. Christ! No more, no less. That's what I'm working so hard at day after day, year after year, doing my best with the energy God so generously gives me."

So there is only one last question to answer … Why not the best? … Why don't we give the best in everything we do?

7 reasons to do your best in everything your hands find to do …

1. God is checking you out … carefully evaluating your performance.

Colossians 3:22 in the Message Bible says:

"Servants, do what you're told by your earthly masters. And don't just do the minimum that will get you by. Do your best. Work from the heart for your real Master, for God, confident that you'll get paid in full when you come into your inheritance. Keep in mind always that the ultimate Master you're serving is Christ. The sullen servant who does shoddy work will be held responsible. Being a follower of Jesus doesn't cover up bad work."

2. You never know who's discussing your next assignment, promotion or opportunity.

Ephesians 9:15-16 in the Amplified Bible says:

> *"Look carefully then how you walk! Live purposefully and worthily and accurately, not as the unwise and witless, but as wise (sensible, intelligent people), Making the very most of the time [buying up each opportunity], because the days are evil"*

3. Your best efforts in the marketplace will attract attention.

1 Timothy 4:15 in the New Living Translation says:

> *"Give your complete attention to these matters. Throw yourself into your tasks so that everyone will see your progress."*

4. Your focus is apparent to those who marvel at your success.

The best reason to be focused in giving God your best efforts is found in Luke 9:41 in the Message Bible which says:

> *"Jesus said, 'What a generation! No sense of God! No focus to your lives! How many times do I have to go over these things? How much longer do I have to put up with this?'"*

5. Your persistence is recognized.

Revelation 2:2 in the Message Bible says:

"I see what you've done, your hard, hard work, your refusal to quit. I know you can't stomach evil, that you weed out apostolic pretenders. I know your persistence, your courage in my cause that you never wear out."

6. The depth of your character is obvious to others.

Ruth 2:11-12 in the Message Bible says:

"Boaz answered her, 'I've heard all about you—heard about the way you treated your mother-in-law after the death of her husband, and how you left your father and mother and the land of your birth and have come to live among a bunch of total strangers. God reward you well for what you've done—and with a generous bonus besides from God, to whom you've come seeking protection under his wings.'"

7. When you do your best ... someone is observing you ... deciding whether to bring their influence and support into your life.

Psalm 32:8 in the Amplified Bible says:

"I [the Lord] will instruct you and teach you in the way you should go; I will counsel you with My eye upon you."

When you do your best ... the One who wants your best ... is watching you.

I received a praise report recently of *a seed planted to honor God* and of **GOD'S BLESSING RETURNED**.

I THANK GOD for you and your ministry. I have a testimony that will give you encouragement for you to keep on keeping on.

On June 7 … I went to the post office and mailed off my **Payday Is Coming** *seed of $100.00.*

The same day Joy on your prayer team called and asked if I needed prayer. I said **YES** *with excitement, both for my VA Disability increase and a career job opportunity with the county government. I had applied for several positions and heard nothing yet knew they had pulled my resume and application and forwarded it to the hiring manager. We prayed together and* **agreed on both to come to pass in God's timing**.

Within two months, **God heard and answered my prayer**.

(1) My VA disability was increased from 50% to 70% and has already been deposited into my checking account.

(2) At the same time I had an interview for the government position that Joy and I prayed for with ALL benefits, retirement and perks. It is a two-round interview and I have my FAITH in GOD that if this is His will for my life, I will re-

ceive the job to help fund Kingdom business.

Brother Harold and Sister Bev, THANK YOU so much for your obedience and your ability to **not only hear GOD but execute what HE has spoken** *and given you to do to advance HIS KINGDOM. GOD BLESS YOU !!!!*

PLEASE join your FAITH with me that this will be a year of **TOTAL RESTORATION AND DEBT FREE LIVING** *for me and my entire family.*

WE LOVE YOU!!!!

Victoria

Praise God. *He wants to do this same thing for you …* and He will **if you choose to honor Him with the best you can give**.

(Praise report edited for length.)

Day 10

God Is Checking You Out

I read about you in scripture this morning … I was reading Proverbs 10 since this is the 10th day of the month … when I came across verse 22 in the Amplified Bible which says:

> *"The blessing of the Lord—it makes [truly] rich, and He adds no sorrow with it [neither does toiling increase it]."*

Personalize it … Shelia … Michelle … Jana …

> *"The blessing of the Lord—it makes <<Your Name>> [truly] rich, and He adds no sorrow with it [neither does toiling increase it]."*

Isn't that a great way to begin today's teaching … now let's discuss the fact … that … God is **checking you out …**

God is very specific in His instructions.

Deuteronomy 8:1 says:

> *"All the commandments which I command thee*

this day shall ye observe to do …"

In Hebrews 8:5 we are told that God used the children of Israel as an example for us.

There is a very good reason that you and I should obey His directions.

Deuteronomy 8:1 continues by saying:

"… that ye may live, and multiply, and go in and possess the land which the LORD."

When it comes to wealth and/or opportunity *God checks us out* … to determine our response to His Word and His commands.

Deuteronomy 8:2 says:

"And thou shalt remember all the way which the LORD thy God led thee these forty years in the wilderness, to humble thee, and to prove thee, to know what was in thine heart, whether thou wouldest keep his commandments, or no."

The New Living Translation of Deuteronomy 8:2 says:

"Remember how the Lord your God led you through the wilderness for these forty years, humbling you and testing you to prove your character, and to find out whether or not you would obey his commands."

It's easy to follow God when things are good … _**but the real measure of your faith is how you act and react when times are tough**_.

In the midst of adversity **God wants to make sure that you're** _depending_ on Him _to deliver you from every attack of the enemy_ … and even from the success you will enjoy through obedience.

Deuteronomy 8:3 says:

> _"… that he might make thee know that man doth not live by bread only, but by every word that proceedeth out of the mouth of the LORD doth man live."_

Our obedience to Him and His word is **an absolute prerequisite** _on our journey to the rich and satisfying life mentioned in John 10:10._

Deuteronomy 8:6 says:

> _"Therefore thou shalt keep the commandments of the LORD thy God, to walk in his ways, and to fear him."_

When you obey God … follow His instructions … **act on His promises**, then the Lord will … as it says in Deuteronomy 8:7-9 … bring you:

> _"… into a good land, a land of brooks of water, of fountains and depths that spring out of valleys and hills; A land of wheat, and barley, and vines,_

*and fig trees, and pomegranates; a land of oil ol-
ive, and honey; A land wherein thou shalt eat
bread without scarceness, thou shalt not lack
any thing in it ..."*

You **may have been traveling through enemy terri-
tory** but *God is going to bring you into a fresh place*
... **where every need will be met *and you will
LACK FOR NOTHING***.

I personally like that phrase ... in fact, lay claim to it
... make it a part of your daily confession ... personalize it.

I WILL LACK FOR NOTHING.

HAROLD HERRING WILL LACK FOR NOTHING ...
Beverly ... Jim ... Martha ...

HAROLD AND BEV HERRING WILL LACK FOR
NOTHING.

That's sounds pretty good ... ***but it gets even better
... when you remember the Lord thy God and what
He's done for you***.

Check out Deuteronomy 8: 12-13. It says:

*"Lest when thou hast eaten and art full, and hast
built goodly houses, and dwelt therein; And
when thy herds and thy flocks multiply, and thy
silver and thy gold is multiplied, and all that thou
hast is multiplied."*

You will have a good house ... **you may have left behind a house in Egypt during your time of bondage to debt** ... but <u>rejoice you're going to have</u> <u>"goodly houses."</u>

Notice the **scripture doesn't just say that you're going to have a house** ... *it says that you're going to have "houses."* Are you hearing this?

Plus ... the two verses also **promise that everything you have will be multiplied**. <u>Silver and gold will be</u> <u>multiplied to you.</u>

I don't know about you ... but I like the Word multiplied. When it comes to **money and possessions** ... *multiplication is definitely better than addition*.

I also like the Message Bible translation of verses 11-13:

> *<u>"Make sure you don't forget God, your God, by</u>* *<u>not keeping his commandments, his rules and</u>* *<u>regulations that I command you today</u>. Make* *sure that when you eat and are satisfied, build* *pleasant houses and settle in, see your herds* *and flocks flourish and **more and more money*** *<u>**come in**, watch your standard of living going up</u>* *<u>and up</u>."*

It says that obedient children are going to have "more and more money" coming into your life. But once again, in Deuteronomy 8:14 **we're reminded that we have what we have and we will give what we give**

… <u>not by our own hand</u> … but because of the Lord. **<u>We must always remember … what the Lord has done for us</u>.**

Deuteronomy 8:14 says:

> *"Then thine heart be lifted up, and thou forget."*

Deuteronomy 8:14 in the Message Bible says it a little clearer:

> *"Make sure you don't become so full of yourself and your things that you forget God, your God."*

When it comes to our success in life … we must also remember that <u>it's not by our efforts</u>.

Deuteronomy 8:17 says:

> *"And thou say in thine heart, My power and the might of mine hand hath gotten me this wealth."*

The people of Israel lived primarily in an agrarian society at this time. ***People earned money by using their hands.*** This verse is admonishing us to remember that *<u>we have what we have not</u> because **of who we are or what we've done** but because of who God is as He works in and through us.*

Once again, we're told to remember … **where our blessings and benefits come from**.

Deuteronomy 8:18 says:

> ***"But thou shalt remember** the LORD thy God:*

for it is he that giveth thee power to get wealth, that he may establish his covenant which he sware unto thy fathers, as it is this day."

Unfortunately, **as many believers become success-ful they forget ... how they got where they are**.

I understand that you may have worked hard to get where you are ... but I also know that it was <u>the Lord who gave you</u> ... <u>a brain to think with</u> ... <u>the strength of body to work</u> ... **the health to function properly ... and the skills to create possibilities**.

In short, <u>**we are who we are**</u> ... <u>**and where we are**</u> ... <u>***because of who is in us***</u>.

We <u>**tend to forget why we are where we are**</u> ... **those who've helped and blessed us along the way**.

But let us always remember ... that God is checking us out.

Hallelujah!! Amen.

Day 11

7 Ways to Be Perceptive About His Precepts

There is something amazing about unconditional love.

Interestingly enough, you can often find a good example in a dog's love.

A dog wants to please you. They love you no matter what … listen to every word you say and never complain.

Truthfully, I'm not sure what these musings have to do with the next text. Maybe *we should live to please God, show our unconditional loyalty without complaining … because when it's all said and done … dogs don't have such a bad life … at least not at our house.*

But let's move on to today's teaching … Psalm 103:17 in the Amplified Bible says:

> *"But the mercy and loving-kindness of the Lord are from everlasting to everlasting upon those who reverently and worshipfully fear Him, and His righteousness is to children's children."*

The Contemporary English Version of Psalm 103:17 says:

"The LORD is always kind to those who worship him, and he keeps his promises to their descendants."

Do you want to experience God's kindness to you … then worship Him.

Obey His Word and follow His percepts.

The New International Version of Psalm 103:17 says:

"But from everlasting to everlasting the LORD's love is with those who fear him and his righteousness with their children's children-with those who keep his covenant and remember to obey his precepts."

I find it interesting that *21 of the 24 times the Word precepts is used in the King James Version of the Bible … it just happens to be in Psalm 119.*

According to *Strong's Concordance* the Hebrew word for *percepts* is most often translated as:

"command or commandments."

The scripture is simple … if we keep God's commandments … His instructions … if we longingly worship and fear Him … if we seek His presence … *then He will be kind to us and keep His promises to even our children and grandchildren.*

Here are seven ways to be perceptive about God's precepts.

1.   We Should Meditate on His Precepts.

Psalm 119:15 says:

> *"I will meditate on Your precepts and have respect to Your ways [the paths of life marked out by Your law]."*

What does God want us to do with His precepts?

Psalm 119:15 in the Message Bible makes it clear enough:

> *"I will study your teachings and follow your footsteps."*

2.   We Should Observe His Precepts.

Psalm 119:4 in the Amplified Bible says:

> *"You have commanded us to keep Your precepts, that we should observe them diligently."*

As long as you follow His instructions and seek His presence, then you will be blessed.

2 Chronicles 26:5 says:

> *"… as long as he sought the LORD, God made him to prosper."*

When we obey His Word … follow His precepts and commands … then we will be rewarded for our obedience and loving Him.

3.   If We Long for His Precepts … We Will Enjoy A Good Life.

We should have an insatiable appetite for His Word … always ready to dig in for this nugget or that. **God truly wants to give us a life worth living.**

Psalm 119:40 in the Amplified Bible says:

"Behold, I long for Your precepts; in Your righteousness give me renewed life."

4.   Hold Fast to His Precepts Even in The Midst Of Adversity.

Psalm 119:69 in the Amplified Bible says:

"The arrogant and godless have put together a lie against me, but I will keep Your precepts with my whole heart."

You can't control what other people say, think or do … but you are in complete control of your own mind, mouth and destiny.

The Message Bible translation of Psalm 119:69 *tells us exactly what we should do when we're being lied about and mistreated by others*. The Word says:

"The godless spread lies about me, but I focus my attention on what you are saying."

Wow … this is powerful. Our natural reaction to being lied about and mistreated is to respond with retaliation.

When someone has done you wrong … the world says … don't get mad, get even. Others say … don't get even, get ahead. But that's not what the Word of God says to do … or even think.

If we focus on Him and what He's saying … we will forget about them.

We must adopt the attitude found in Psalms 119:87 in the New Living Translation which says:

"They almost finished me off, but I refused to abandon your commandments."

5.   He Will Give Us a Helping Hand as We Follow His Precepts.

Have you ever tried to walk down a railroad track balancing yourself on just one track? *You can make it for a short while but then you will inevitably fall.*

However, if you join hands with someone walking on the other track … you can go miles and miles since you have their helping hand you to balance. *The same is true with God; He will be your helping hand as you obey His instructions.*

Psalm 119:73 in the Amplified Bible says:

"Let Your hand be ready to help me, for I have chosen Your precepts."

6. We Will Walk in Freedom When We Follow His Precepts.

Psalm 119:45 in the New Living Translation says:

"I will walk in freedom, for I have devoted myself to your commandments."

We enjoy personal freedom, peace and prosperity because of our obedience to His precepts and instructions.

2 Corinthians 3:17 in the New Living Translation says:

"For the Lord is the Spirit, and wherever the Spirit of the Lord is, there is freedom."

7. We Will Be Blessed When We Follow His Precepts.

Psalm 119:56 in the Amplified Bible says:

"This I have had [as the gift of Your grace and as my reward]: that I have kept Your precepts [hearing, receiving, loving, and obeying them]."

When we follow His percepts, we aren't just blessed on occasion ... we create a blessing flow

in our lives.

The Contemporary English Version of Psalm 119:56 says:

> *"You have blessed me because I have always followed your teachings."*

There is one final thought I want to leave with you ... and it's found in Galatians 6:7 in the Amplified Bible where it says:

> *"Do not be deceived and deluded and misled; God will not allow Himself to be sneered at (scorned, disdained, or mocked by mere pretensions or professions, or by His precepts being set aside.) [He inevitably deludes himself who attempts to delude God.] For whatever a man sows, that and that only is what he will reap."*

The key phrase I want to share with you in closing is simply this: **God will not allow His precepts to be sneered at, scorned, disdained, mocked or set aside.**

If you want to live a long, good life ... follow His precepts and instructions.

Psalm 1:2 in the Amplified Bible says:

> *"But his delight and desire are in the law of the Lord, and on His law (the precepts, the instructions, the teachings of God) he habitually medi-*

tates (ponders and studies) by day and by night."

And just for the record, I first labeled this teaching as, "A Dog's Life Isn't So Bad After All."

Day 12

7 Reasons It's Smart to Delight in Him

Have you ever had God lead you on a journey through the scriptures? It's happened to me a number of times …

most recently, as I read Psalm 37:4 which says:

> *"Delight thyself also in the LORD: and he shall give thee the desires of thine heart."*

I will confess to you that I got excited studying the scriptures and teaching on the desires of my heart. I was imagining all sorts of possibilities.

However, God had something else in mind. *He directed me to read every scripture in the King James Version of the Bible that contained the word <u>delight</u>.*

Just for the record … eighty-two scriptures fall into that category. I knew He wanted me to write about how, why and what happens when we delight in Him.

According to dictionary.com the word delight means:

"a high degree of pleasure or enjoyment; joy; something that gives great pleasure"

According to *Strong's Concordance* the Hebrew word for *delight* is `a nag (H6026) and it means:

"to be of dainty habit, be pampered; to be happy about, take exquisite delight; to make merry over."

When we obey His instructions ... good things are coming our way.

Numbers 14:8 says:

"If the LORD delight in us, then he will bring us into this land, and give it us; a land which floweth with milk and honey."

When God delights in our worship ... our righteousness ... He protects and provides for us.

Psalm 18:18-20 says:

"They prevented me in the day of my calamity: but the LORD was my stay. He brought me forth also into a large place; he delivered me, because he delighted in me. The LORD rewarded me according to my righteousness; according to the cleanness of my hands hath he recompensed me."

2 Samuel 22:19-21 in the New Living Translation says:

"They attacked me at a moment when I was in

distress, but the Lord supported me. He led me to a place of safety; he rescued me because he delights in me. The Lord rewarded me for doing right; he restored me because of my innocence."

As I was reading and taking notes on the 82 scriptures with the word delight … *it became clear to me … that my focus was not to be on desire but on our delight in Him.*

Here are seven reasons it's smart to delight in Him.

1. You delight in the Lord by being in His presence.

Job 22:26 says:

"For then shalt thou have thy delight in the Almighty, and shalt lift up thy face unto God."

When someone is important to you … *you delight in their presence.* That's how I feel about my fine wife Bev, my parents, my sugars and grandsugars.

I want to be with them … *not because of what they can or are doing for me.* I just want to be in their presence.

I want to spend time with them … *talk with them* … go places with them … *do things with them.* I want to be with them continually … especially, my fine wife.

That's how our Heavenly Father wants us to feel

about Him.

2. Delight in His Word ... by following His instructions.

Many of the scriptures I read discuss how we're to delight in His instructions. I feel led to share five of them with you.

First, Psalm 1:2 says:

> *"But his delight is in the law of the LORD; and in his law doth he meditate day and night."*

Second, Psalm 112:1 says:

> *"Praise ye the LORD. Blessed is the man that feareth the LORD, that delighteth greatly in his commandments."*

Third, Psalm 40:8 says:

> *"I delight to do thy will, O my God: yea, thy law is within my heart."*

Fourth, Psalm 119:16 says:

> *"I will delight myself in thy statutes: I will not forget thy word."*

Fifth, Psalm 119:47 says:

> *"And I will delight myself in thy commandments,*

which I have loved."

And when you delight in His Word ... you will be pleased.

Romans 7:22 is the only time delight is found in the New Testament. It says:

> *"For I delight in the law of God after the inward man."*

Romans 7:22 in the New Living Translation says:

> *"Your laws please me; they give me wise advice."*

When we delight in the Lord ... *and obey His instructions ... it makes Him* ... Happy, Happy, Happy.

3. You delight in the Lord by spending time in prayer.

I love my fine wife Bev ... but if the only time I talked to her was for two hours on Sunday morning and an hour on Wednesday night ... we wouldn't have much of a relationship.

We need to talk to Him ... delight in Him ... on a daily basis.

Proverbs 15:8 says:

> *"The sacrifice of the wicked is an abomination to*

the LORD: but the prayer of the upright is his delight."

Isaiah 58:2 says:

"Yet they seek me daily, and delight to know my ways, as a nation that did righteousness, and forsook not the ordinance of their God: they ask of me the ordinances of justice; they take delight in approaching to God."

If you know something is a delight to the Lord ... *wouldn't it be spiritually smart* ... to do what He delights in? *Pray.*

4. When you delight in Him ... you have a healthier, peaceful life.

Psalm 119:92 says:

"Unless thy law had been my delights, I should then have perished in mine affliction."

Psalm 119:92 in the New Living Translation says:

"If your instructions hadn't sustained me with joy, I would have died in my misery."

Let's see ... *be sick, live in misery* or *delight in Him.* The choice is obvious.

5. Delighting in Him is the best remedy for pressure and stress.

Psalm 119:143 says:

> *"Trouble and anguish have taken hold on me: yet thy commandments are my delights."*

If things in the workplace are causing you stress … *spend more time proportionately delighting in Him* … His presence and obeying His instructions.

One more thing … if you delight in the Lord … *He will not only relieve your anguish* … He will correct you … where *and as needed*.

Proverbs 3:12 says:

> *"For whom the LORD loveth he correcteth; even as a father the son in whom he delighteth."*

6.   When you're honest and do what's right in business … He delights in you.

The scripture is very clear … He delights in us when we practice ethical business habits … such as not cutting corners.

Proverbs 11:1 says:

> *"A false balance is abomination to the LORD: but a just weight is his delight."*

Proverbs 12:22 says:

> *"Lying lips are abomination to the LORD: but*

they that deal truly are his delight."

Proverbs 16:13 says:

"Righteous lips are the delight of kings; and they love him that speaketh right."

7. When the Lord delights in you ... He will empower you to bring forth justice and judgment.

Isaiah 42:1 says:

"Behold my servant, whom I uphold; mine elect, in whom my soul delighteth; I have put my spirit upon him: he shall bring forth judgment to the Gentiles."

Malachi 3:12 says:

"And all nations shall call you blessed: for ye shall be a delightsome land, saith the LORD of hosts."

One final observation ... and it's found in Psalm 37:23 in the Amplified Bible which says:

"The steps of a [good] man are directed and es-tablished by the Lord when He delights in his way [and He busies Himself with his every step]."

When we delight in Him ... He will direct our path ...

and truthfully, that should be the desire of all our hearts.

Psalm 37:4 which says:

"Delight thyself also in the LORD: and he shall give thee the desires of thine heart."

Day

13

7 Things About Your Abundant Benefits

Have you ever been around Christians who seemed like they were weaned on prune juice?

You know the kind I'm talking about … wound so tight … *they'd spin forever if they were a top.*

I've actually had conversations with people who feel that's the proper demeanor for a believer … *somber and introspective.* However, that's not what the Word of God says.

Deuteronomy 28:47-48 says:

"If you do not serve the Lord your God with joy and enthusiasm for the abundant benefits you have received, you will serve your enemies whom the Lord will send against you. You will be left hungry, thirsty, naked, and lacking in everything …"

1.   Serve the Lord your God with joy.

Joy is an inward work. *It comes from having an inner peace birthed due to obedience and trust.*

Proverbs 16:20 in the New Living Translation says:

"Those who listen to instruction will prosper; those who trust the Lord will be joyful."

If you listen to and obey His instructions … you will prosper. The verse doesn't say … may, might, could or should … *it says you WILL prosper.* And the verse also says that you will be joyful.

Deuteronomy 28:47 in the Amplified Bible says:

"Because you did not serve the Lord your God with joyfulness of [mind and] heart [in gratitude] for the abundance of all [with which He had blessed you]."

"Of the mind" is what you're thinking … "*of the heart*" *is what you're doing.* When the mind and heart line up in obedience to His instructions … there is joy in your midst.

2.   Serve the Lord your God with enthusiasm.

Everything you do … *should be done as unto the Lord and with enthusiasm.*

Ephesians 6:7 in the New Living Translation says:

"Work with enthusiasm, as though you were

working for the Lord rather than for people."

Here are three power thoughts *to help you understand more clearly* what enthusiasm really means … and I've shared a couple of them before.

First, the last four letters of the word "enthusiasm" are "-iasm" which stand for "I am sold myself."

Second, **according to Latin and Greek dictionaries, the word "enthusiasm" literally means "God within."**

When you can allow the greater one within you **to stir your greatest desire for excellence, you will have all the motivation you need**.

Third, enthusiasm is one of the six things that God wants you to excel at.

2 Corinthians 8:7 in the New Living Translation says:

> *"Since you excel in so many ways—in your faith, your gifted speakers, your knowledge, your enthusiasm, and your love from us —I want you to excel also in this gracious act of giving."*

3.   Praise the Lord your God with gratitude for the abundant benefits you have received.

One of the most quoted verses in scripture is Psalm 35:27 which says:

"Let them shout for joy, and be glad, that favour my righteous cause: yea, let them say continually, Let the LORD be magnified, which hath pleasure in the prosperity of his servant."

I've asked hundreds of audiences around the world to quote the next verse and no one has ever been able to do so.

Psalm 35:28 in the Amplified Bible says:

"And my tongue shall talk of Your righteousness, rightness, and justice, and of [my reasons for] Your praise all the day long."

Our attitude of gratitude for what God has done for us … *His amazing benefits* … should be a continual state of mind and speech.

The Message Bible translation of Psalm 35:28 says:

"I'll tell the world how great and good you are, I'll shout Hallelujah all day, every day."

4. Joyfully worship Him.

When I think about joyfully worshipping our great God Jehovah … the first things that come to my mind are the lines from two songs.

The first is "This Joy I Have" by Shirley Ceasar.

This joy that I have … the world didn't give it to me

and the world can't take it away. The song goes on to say that robbers can't take it away … repo men can't take it away. Hallelujah!!

The second song is actually based on Psalm 30:5 which in the Amplified Bible says:

"For His anger is but for a moment, but His favor is for a lifetime or in His favor is life. Weeping may endure for a night, but joy comes in the morning."

Joy comes in the morning. *Joy follows weeping when He is at the core of our existence* … when we are at peace with Him … *worshipping Him for all He has done, is doing and will continue to do.*

5.   Honor the Lord with your whole heart.

The word honor is in the King James Version of the Bible a total of *178 times* and the New Living Translation a total of *366 times*.

If God says something once … I believe it's important to Him and us. However, *if he says something hundreds of times* … we're better pay attention to what He's saying.

1 Samuel 2:30 in the New Living Translation says:

"Therefore, the Lord, the God of Israel, says: I promised that your branch of the tribe of Levi would always be my priests. But I will honor

those who honor me, and I will despise those who think lightly of me."

Honor is respect. *Honor is giving credit where credit is due.*

Honor is important to God … *so it should be important to us as well.*

Our prayer should be the same as what's written in Psalm 86:11 in the Amplified Bible which says:

"Teach me Your way, O Lord, that I may walk and live in Your truth; direct and unite my heart [solely, reverently] to fear and honor Your name."

6.   Praise the Lord for making you wealthy.

1 Corinthians 1:26 in the New Living Translation says:

"Remember, dear brothers and sisters, that few of you were wise in the world's eyes or powerful or wealthy when God called you."

Always remember who made you wealthy.

Deuteronomy 8:18 says:

"But thou shalt remember the LORD thy God: for it is he that giveth thee power to get wealth, that he may establish his covenant which he sware unto thy fathers, as it is this day."

Praise the Lord for it is He who gives you wealth and the power to get it.

Deuteronomy 8:17 in the Amplified Bible says:

"And beware lest you say in your [mind and] heart, My power and the might of my hand have gotten me this wealth."

At the time the scripture was written people lived in an agrarian society … *where they worked with their hands* … so this verse takes on added significance.

Your wealth is not because of what you've done … *but rather what He's done and is doing through and in you.*

7.   Practice the first six reasons or experience the consequence.

Deuteronomy 28:48 in the Contemporary English Version says:

"He will send enemies to attack you and make you their slaves. Then you will live in poverty with nothing to eat, drink, or wear, and your owners will work you to death."

When people aren't appreciative or complain about what God's done for them … it doesn't make Him a happy camper.

Numbers 11:1 says:

"And when the people complained, it displeased the LORD: and the LORD heard it; and his anger was kindled; and the fire of the LORD burnt among them, and consumed them that were in the uttermost parts of the camp."

What displeases the Lord? Complaining!

The scripture is very clear that God feels complaining is evil. It says God also got angry. <u>That's probably not something we want to do</u> … *make God angry*.

So my suggestion is that <u>you focus on the first six reasons to be thankful</u> so you *never have to experience the reality of number seven.*

Day 14

7 Keys to 20/20 Spiritual Vision

Here are 7 keys to having 20/20 spiritual vision.

1.   Evil thoughts change the view of what you're seeing.

Genesis 3:5 in the New Living Translation says:

> *"God knows that your eyes will be opened as soon as you eat it, and you will be like God, knowing both good and evil."*

The Tree of the Knowledge of Good and Evil had not changed … *it still was the same except one major thing. Eve's perception of that tree changed by the words that came out of the devil's mouth.*

Have you ever wondered why Eve didn't think it was strange that a snake was talking? *Don't know, not suggesting anything … just asking a question.*

Back to the teaching … *sin entered the Garden of Eden when Eve and Adam began to see the Tree of the Knowledge of Good and Evil differently* than they'd ever seen it before.

The thoughts suggested by the enemy changed their view of that particular tree. *Now the Garden couple was looking at a tree they'd seen for years with a covetous eye.*

Moral of this story … *never allow others to change the reality of what the Word or presence of God reveals to you.*

2. When we're blinded by our circumstances … we can't see our answer right in front of us.

Genesis 21:19 in the New Living Translation says:

> *"Then God opened Hagar's eyes, and she saw a well full of water. She quickly filled her water container and gave the boy a drink."*

God told Abraham that he and Sarah were going to have a child. *After a few years Sarah decided to help God out.* She gave Abraham Hagar who then had Ishmael. *Later, Sarah had Isaac just as God had promised.*

Then trouble happened. Sarah went to Abraham and told him to get rid of Hagar and her son because they were laughing at her. *Abraham listened but he didn't want to do it.*

Genesis 21:12 says:

> *"Let it not be grievous in your sight because of the lad and the bondwoman and all that Sarah said unto thee. Harken to her voice for in Isaac shall thy seed be called."*

In verse 14 we see Abraham rose up and gave them some bread and water *and sent then out.*

After the bread and water were gone … they were out in the wilderness. Hagar set the boy down and cried out to God … saying, *"Lord, I can't watch this boy die."*

An angel came to her and said in verse 17:

> *"What aileth thee Hagar? Fear not for God hath heard the voice of the lad where he is. Arise, lift up the lad and hold him in thine hand for I will make him a great nation."*

Genesis 21:19 in the Amplified Bible says:

> *"Then God opened her eyes and she saw a well of water; and she went and filled the [empty] bottle with water and caused the youth to drink."*

The water had been there all the time … *but she was so blinded by her circumstances that she couldn't see it!*

There is opportunity in front of you right now … *but you may not see it … because you have been hypno-*

tized by your circumstances … or blinded by the thoughts of the enemy.

3. Never let what you see limit or eliminate your deliverance.

2 Kings 7:2 in the New Living Translation says:

> *"The officer assisting the king said to the man of God, 'That couldn't happen even if the Lord opened the windows of heaven!' But Elisha replied, 'You will see it happen with your own eyes, but you won't be able to eat any of it!'"*

In various translations, the officer is referred to as a "lord"; "captain" and "chief officer." One translation refers to the officer assisting the king as a wise man. *Truthfully, he must have been an unwise man to ever question God and His ability to open the windows of heaven and bring deliverance to the land.*

The officer's problem is that he had lived in lack so long that he could not imagine being delivered from the famine or the attack of the enemy. He limited God and, as a result, it ultimately cost him his life.

2 Kings 7:17 in the Amplified Bible says:

> *"… the [starving] people trampled him in the gate [as they struggled to get through for food], and he died, as the man of God had foretold when the king came down to him."*

Regardless of how desperate your circumstances may be ... never question ... *nor doubt God's ability to bring instant deliverance to your situation.*

4. When you see with your spiritual eyes ... you'll realize you're never alone.

One morning, the prophet Elisha's servant Gehazi got up early to go pick up Krispy Kreme Doughnuts and a copy of the *USA Today* newspaper for his master and mentor. (Teasing)

What Gehazi saw with his natural eyes ... *made him feel there was real trouble in the city.*

2 Kings 6:15 says:

> *"And when the servant of the man of God was risen early, and gone forth, behold, an host compassed the city both with horses and chariots. And his servant said unto him, Alas, my master! how shall we do?"*

Fortunately, for Gehazi ... *Elisha saw things as they were and not as they appeared to be.*

2 Kings 6:16-17 says:

> *"And he answered, Fear not: for they that be with us are more than they that be with them. And Elisha prayed, and said, LORD, I pray thee, open his eyes, that he may see. And the LORD opened the eyes of the young man; and he saw:*

and, behold, the mountain was full of horses and chariots of fire round about Elisha."

No matter the adversity you're facing ... *real or imagined* ... you're never alone. And more importantly, *you never will be as long as you put Him first.*

5. You may be looking at your answer ... but not recognize it.

I can't speak for you ... but there have been times in my life ... *too many to count* ... where I expected God to answer my prayers in one way ... *but it came from a totally different and almost always, unsuspected direction.*

Luke 24:16 in the Message Bible says:

"That same day two of them were walking to the village Emmaus, about seven miles out of Jerusalem. They were deep in conversation, going over all these things that had happened. In the middle of their talk and questions, Jesus came up and walked along with them. But they were not able to recognize who he was."

I can tell you these two men weren't discussing the three years of miracles *or the teachings of Jesus ... they were focused on their view of what happened with the betrayal, arrest, crucifixion and resurrection.*

How can I be so sure?

Luke 24:18 in the New Living Translation says:

"Then one of them, Cleopas, replied, 'You must be the only person in Jerusalem who hasn't heard about all the things that have happened there the last few days.'"

These men were talking about what had happened instead of focusing on what was going to happen.

6. What you see ... will determine your destiny.

In Numbers 13, twelve men personally chosen by Moses went to spy out the Promised Land.

Ten of them came back with a negative report with stories about the fortified cities and giants among them. The ten spies even said in Numbers 13:33:

"And there we saw the giants, the sons of Anak, which come of the giants: and we were in our own sight as grasshoppers, and so we were in their sight."

The last half of this verse tells the story. *"... and we were in our own sight as grasshoppers, and so we were in their sight."*

The ten spies by their own admission saw themselves as grasshoppers compared to the giants ... *who came to view the children of Israel ... the same way they saw themselves.*

However, things were different with Caleb and Joshua *who saw beyond the giants to the promise of the land God was giving them.*

Numbers 13:30 says:

> *"Caleb quieted the people before Moses, and said, Let us go up at once and possess it; we are well able to conquer it."*

Twelve people saw the same things ... *but two of them saw it differently* and as a result were able to enter the Promised Land.

Is what you see determining whether or not you will enter into the promises of God?

7.   God will allow you to see your deliverance.

Exodus 14:13 in the Amplified Bible says:

> *"Moses told the people, Fear not; stand still (firm, confident, undismayed) and see the salvation of the Lord which He will work for you today. For the Egyptians you have seen today you shall never see again."*

No matter what you're facing ... DO NOT BE AFRAID.

Your Great God Jehovah wants you to STAND FIRM in your confession of faith *because He will bring your deliverance to you ... today.* Hallelujah!!!

Day 15

7 Keys to His Blessing Flow

Have you ever wondered why you were born?

Have you ever wondered what your job is here on planet earth?

Have you ever wondered what it really takes to experience the blessings of God?

Have you ever wondered if there was one verse that would explain *what you need to do* … in order to experience the blessings of God?

Would you like to know the 7 keys to walking in God's blessing flow?

The answers to these questions and so much more are found in 1 Peter 3:8-12 in the Message Bible translation which says:

> *"Summing up: Be agreeable, be sympathetic, be loving, be compassionate, be humble. That goes for all of you, no exceptions. No retaliation. No sharp-tongued sarcasm. Instead, bless—that's*

your job, to bless. You'll be a blessing and also get a blessing."

Personalize this verse by inserting your name.

"… Instead, bless—that's <<Your Name>>'s job, to bless. <<Your Name>> will be a blessing and also get a blessing."

Let's continue with 1 Peter 3:8-12 in verse 10:

"Whoever wants to embrace life and see the day fill up with good, here's what you do: Say nothing evil or hurtful; Snub evil and cultivate good; run after peace for all you're worth. God looks on all this with approval, listening and responding well to what he's asked; But he turns his back on those who do evil things."

Let's look at the beginning of verse 8 again.

"Summing up: Be agreeable, be sympathetic, be loving, be compassionate, be humble …"

Immediately the Word reveals five things that you and I are to "be" if we want to experience His blessings.

First, be agreeable.

Proverbs 16:3 in the Amplified Bible gives us the key to being agreeable. Do God's will!

"Roll your works upon the Lord [commit and trust

them wholly to Him; He will cause your thoughts to become agreeable to His will, and] so shall your plans be established and succeed."

Second, be sympathetic.

Luke 6:36 in the Amplified Bibles reveals the key to being sympathetic.

"So be merciful (sympathetic, tender, responsive, and compassionate) even as your Father is [all these]."

Third, be loving.

Psalm 109:16 in the New Century Version reveals how "not" to be loving.

"He did not remember to be loving. He hurt the poor, the needy, and those who were sad until they were nearly dead."

Whereas, the message of 1 Corinthians 16:14 in the New International Readers Version is clear:

"Be loving in everything you do."

Fourth, be compassionate.

Philippians 2:1 in the New Living Translation offers excellent advice.

"[Have the Attitude of Christ] Is there any en-

couragement from belonging to Christ? Any comfort from his love? Any fellowship together in the Spirit? Are your hearts tender and compassionate?"

Fifth, be humble.

Psalm 69:32 in the New Living Translation reveals an excellent reason to be humble.

"The humble will see their God at work and be glad. Let all who seek God's help be encouraged."

After the scripture tells us what to be … it reveals the 7 keys to experiencing His blessing flow.

 # 1   Say nothing evil or hurtful.

Ephesians 4:29 in the Amplified Bible says:

"Let no foul or polluting language, nor evil word nor unwholesome or worthless talk [ever] come out of your mouth, but only such [speech] as is good and beneficial to the spiritual progress of others, as is fitting to the need and the occasion, that it may be a blessing and give grace (God's favor) to those who hear it."

 # 2   Snub evil.

Psalm 4:4 in the Amplified Bible says:

"Be angry [or stand in awe] and sin not; com-

mune with your own hearts upon your beds and be silent (sorry for the things you say in your hearts). Selah [pause, and calmly think of that]!"

3　Cultivate good.

In Psalm 34:14 in the New International Version we're not only told to turn from evil we're instructed to do good.

"Turn from evil and do good; seek peace and pursue it."

4　Pursue peace for all you're worth.

You may never have run track and field in your entire life *... you might not be able to run across the room without getting out of breath ...* but there are some things we definitely need *to run to* or *run from.*

2 Timothy 2:22 in the New Living Translation says:

"Run from anything that stimulates youthful lusts. Instead, pursue righteous living, faithfulness, love, and peace. Enjoy the companionship of those who call on the Lord with pure hearts."

5　Know that God will approve.

You must serve God with the right kind of attitude in order to be approved by Him.

Romans 14:18 in the New Living Translation says:

"If you serve Christ with this attitude, you will please God, and others will approve of you, too."

Not only do we need to have the right attitude to please God and position ourselves for His blessing flow ... we must be willing to be a hard worker as well.

2 Timothy 2:15 in the New Living Translation says:

"[An Approved Worker] Work hard so you can present yourself to God and receive his approval. Be a good worker, one who does not need to be ashamed and who correctly explains the word of truth."

6   Listen to what He Asks.

The scripture is filled with great reasons why you should always listen to and do what God asks ... one which is found in Deuteronomy 28:12-13 in the Message Bible:

"God will throw open the doors of his sky vaults and pour rain on your land on schedule and bless the work you take in hand. You will lend to many nations but you yourself won't have to take out a loan. God will make you the head, not the tail; you'll always be the top dog, never the bottom dog, as you obediently listen to and diligently keep the commands of God, your God, that I am commanding you today."

7   Get the job done and do it well.

Galatians 6:4 in the New Living Translation says:

> *"Pay careful attention to your own work, for then you will get the satisfaction of a job well done, and you won't need to compare yourself to anyone else."*

One more time let's look at part of 1 Peter 3:8 in the The Message translation:

> *"Summing up: ... bless—that's your job, to bless. You'll be a blessing and also get a blessing ..."*

When you make a concentrated effort on being what He wants you to be and doing or not doing what He instructs you to do ... then you have positioned yourself to receive His blessings.

It's just that simple.

Day 16

7 Ways to Build Strong Faith

Are you expecting a promise from God to be fulfilled?

Are you trusting God for a financial breakthrough?

Are you facing seemingly insurmountable odds?

If so, <u>you must make sure that your faith is strong and unmovable</u>.

You must believe *as Abraham and Sarah did* and *stand firm* until your victory appears.

Romans 4:17-22 in the Amplified Bible says:

> *"As it is written, I have made you the father of many nations. [He was appointed our father] in the sight of God in Whom he believed, **Who gives life to the dead and speaks of the non-existent things that [He has foretold and promised] as if they [already] existed**. [For Abraham, **human reason for] hope being gone**, hoped in faith that he should become the father of many nations, as he had been prom-*

ised, So [numberless] shall your descendants be. **He did not weaken in faith when he considered the [utter] impotence of his own body, which was as good as dead because he was about a hundred years** *old, or [when he considered]* **the barrenness of Sarah's [deadened] womb.** *No unbelief or distrust made him waver (doubtingly question) concerning the promise of God,* **but he grew strong** *and* **was empowered by faith as he gave praise and glory to God, fully satisfied and assured that God was able** *and* **mighty to keep His word** *and* **to do what He had promised.** *That is why his faith was credited to him as righteousness (right standing with God)."*

Let's look at 7 ways to build strong faith.

1. Seeing things as they as can be and *eventually will be* and *not as they are right now.*

Two scriptures confirm this point far better than anything I could ever pen.

First, Romans 4:17 in the Message Bible says:

"When everything was hopeless, Abraham believed anyway, deciding to live not on the basis of what he saw he couldn't do but on what God said he would do."

I think about each of you reading this and what God can do in your lives. I personalize Romans 4:17 like this ...

> *"When everything was hopeless, <<Your Name>> believed anyway, deciding to live not on the basis of what <<he/she>> saw <<he/she>> couldn't do but on what God said <<Your Name>> would do."*

Hebrews 11:1 in the Amplified Bible says:

> *"NOW FAITH is the assurance (the confirmation, the title deed) of the things [we] hope for, being the proof of things [we] do not see and the conviction of their reality [faith perceiving as real fact what is not revealed to the senses]."*

2. Realizing your hope for the future is not based on what you perceive with your natural senses.

Your hope is based on His promises found in the Word of God.

Psalm 130:5 in the New Living Translation says:

> *"I am counting on the Lord; yes, I am counting on him. I have put my hope in his word."*

Always remember, no matter the situation ... *there is only one place where you need to place your hope.*

Psalm 39:7 in the New Living Translation says:

> *"And so, Lord, where do I put my hope? My only hope is in you."*

When you put your hope in the Lord … *it should never be your last resort.*

Psalm 25:5 in the New Living Translation says:

> *"Lead me by your truth and teach me, for you are the God who saves me. All day long I put my hope in you."*

Your hope will remove all the doubts of the enemy.

Psalm 94:19 in the New Living Translation says:

> *"When doubts filled my mind, your comfort gave me renewed hope and cheer."*

Your hope in God empowers you with the confidence of His protection.

Job 11:18 in the New Living Translation says:

> *"Having hope will give you courage. You will be protected and will rest in safety."*

Steadfast hope in Him will bring its own reward to you.

Proverbs 23:18 in the New Living Translation says:

> *"You will be rewarded for this; your hope will not be disappointed."*

3. Remembering it's not what the tests show or what the doctor says but rather what the Great Physician says.

Have you ever talked to a couple who've tried to have children for one, two, five or ten years and have given up … or been told by a doctor they'd never have a child?

Frustration and doubt rob them of hope. Can you image how Abraham must have felt?

The scripture in Romans 4:19 in the Message Bible tells us:

> *"Abraham didn't focus on his own impotence and say, 'It's hopeless. This hundred-year-old body could never father a child.' Nor did he survey Sarah's decades of infertility and give up."*

No matter how long you've been dealing with a certain circumstance … your focus should be to never ever give up or doubt the promises in the Word of God.

4. Deciding to never question or doubt what the Word of God says.

Romans 4:20 in the Contemporary English Version says:

> *"But Abraham never doubted or questioned God's promise …"*

You are allowed to question what your wife, husband, children, parents, best friend, employer or even your pastors says ... *but you must NEVER doubt or question the promises of God.*

The people on the list I've just named may unintentionally lie to or disappoint you ... *BUT God is not a man that He should lie.*

Numbers 23:19 in the New Living Translation says:

"God is not a man, so he does not lie. He is not human, so he does not change his mind. Has he ever spoken and failed to act? Has he ever promised and not carried it through?"

5. Giving credit where credit is due to enable you to grow stronger.

It's really simple ... when you give praise and glory to God ... you grow stronger.

Romans 4:20 in the Amplified Bible says:

"... he grew strong and was empowered by faith as he gave praise and glory to God."

Personalize this verse for your life.

"... <<Your Name>> grew strong and was empowered by faith as <<he/she>> gave praise and glory to God."

When you don't give praise and glory to God … something will die inside you.

Acts 12:23 in God's WORD Translation says:

> *"Immediately, an angel from the Lord killed Herod for not giving glory to God. Herod was eaten by maggots, and he died."*

Given the choice … there is only one choice.

6.   Knowing that God is able to meet your every need.

2 Corinthians 9:8 in the New International Readers Version says:

> *"And God is able to shower all kinds of blessings on you. In all things and at all times you will have everything you need. You will do more and more good works."*

Ephesians 3:20 in the New International Readers Version says:

> *"God is able to do far more than we could ever ask for or imagine. He does everything by his power that is working in us."*

No question … God is able and He will do what He says He will do.

7.   Understanding that God will do what He

says He will do ... builds your reputation as a person of strong faith.

Romans 4:21 says:

"And being fully persuaded that, what he had promised, he was able also to perform."

Romans 4:22 in the Contemporary English Version says:

"So God accepted him."

That's what I want ... for God to accept me as a person of strong faith. In fact, that's my prayer for each of us TODAY.

Day 17

7 Questions that Settle the Issue

I'm continually amazed at how *people who teach* against Biblical prosperity and success *hang their logic on three or four scriptures which are totally taken out of context*. I'm not just talking about preachers either.

There are what I call religious folks who take certain scriptures and basically assume that anyone who is or desires to be rich, wealthy and/or successful is greedy *and unconcerned about the well-being of other less fortunate believers and non-believers*.

This same group of people assumes that money changes people.

Let's get this *misunderstood fact* straight immediately.

Money does not change people. *It only allows what lives in a person to be revealed.* Money merely reflects the character of the person once they have money.

My purpose in this teaching is not to refute the naysayers … *but to pose seven questions which establish the scriptural validity of Biblical prosperity.*

1.　If God didn't want you to be prosperous, why would He give you the power to get wealth in the first place?

Deuteronomy 8:18 in the Amplified Bible says:

> *"But you shall [earnestly] remember the Lord your God, for it is He Who gives you power to get wealth, that He may establish His covenant which He swore to your fathers, as it is this day."*

Ecclesiastes 5:19 in the Amplified Bible says:

> *"Also, every man to whom God has given riches and possessions, and the power to enjoy them and to accept his appointed lot and to rejoice in his toil--this is the gift of God [to him]."*

2 Chronicles 26:5 says:

> *"… and as long as he sought the Lord, God made him to prosper."*

2.　If God didn't want you wealthy, then why does He take pleasure in the prosperity of His servants?

Psalm 35:27 says:

> *"Let them shout for joy, and be glad, that favour my righteous cause: yea, let them say contin-*

ually, Let the LORD be magnified, which hath pleasure in the prosperity of his servant."

Does Job 36:11 say …

"If they obey and serve him, they shall spend their days in poverty, and their years in living in lack."

Laughing … no, Job 36:11 says:

"If they obey and serve him, they shall spend their days in prosperity, and their years in pleasures."

If they obey and serve … if they obey and serve … if they obey and serve *"… they shall spend their days in prosperity, and their years in pleasures."*

3. If God didn't want you, one of His children, to be rich, why would He say that the wealth of the sinner is laid up for the righteous?

Proverbs 13:22 says:

"A good man leaveth an inheritance to his children's children: and the wealth of the sinner is laid up for the just."

Ecclesiastes 2:26 in the New Living Translation says:

"God gives wisdom, knowledge, and joy to those who please him. But if a sinner becomes

wealthy, God takes the wealth away and gives it to those who please him. This, too, is meaningless—like chasing the wind."

4.   If God didn't want you to be prosperous, why would He say that if you let Him … He will make you rich?

2 Corinthians 8:9 in the New Living Translation says:

"You know the generous grace of our Lord Jesus Christ. Though he was rich, yet for your sakes he became poor, so that by his poverty he could make you rich."

Isaiah 1:19 in The Living Bible says:

"If you will only let me help you, if you will only obey, then I will make you rich."

5.   If God didn't want you to be wealthy, why would He promise you success and prosperity?

Three scriptures … you need to personalize and confess … until they're as familiar to you as the air you breath.

Deuteronomy 30:9 says:

"And the Lord your God will make you abundantly prosperous in every work of your hand, in the fruit of your body, of your cattle, of your land, for

good; for the Lord will again delight in prospering you, as He took delight in your fathers."

3 John 2 says:

"Beloved, I wish above all things that thou mayest prosper and be in health, even as thy soul prospereth."

Psalm 112:3 says:

"Wealth and riches shall be in his house: and his righteousness endureth for ever."

6. If God didn't want you to be rich, why would He tell you exactly how to become prosperous and successful?

Joshua 1:8 in the Amplified Bible says:

"This Book of the Law shall not depart out of your mouth, but you shall meditate on it day and night, that you may observe and do according to all that is written in it. For then you shall make your way prosperous, and then you shall deal wisely and have good success."

1 Kings 2:3 in the Amplified Bible says:

"Keep the charge of the Lord your God, walk in His ways, keep His statutes, His commandments, His precepts, and His testimonies, as it is written in the Law of Moses, that you may do

*wisely and prosper in all that you do and wher-
ever you turn."*

I'm going to quote 2 Chronicles 26:5 one more time.
The verse says:

*"... as long as he sought the LORD, God made
him to prosper."*

Galatians 6:7 in the Amplified Bible says:

*"Do not be deceived and deluded and misled;
God will not allow Himself to be sneered at
(scorned, disdained, or mocked by mere pretensions or professions, or by His precepts being
set aside.) [He inevitably deludes himself who
attempts to delude God.] For whatever a man
sows, that and that only is what he will reap."*

7.   If God didn't want you to be wealthy, why would He increase your resources so you could give to others that He may be glori-fied?

2 Corinthians 9:10-11 in the New Living Translation
says:

*"For God is the one who provides seed for the
farmer and then bread to eat. In the same way,
he will provide and increase your resources and
then produce a great harvest of generosity in
you. Yes, you will be enriched in every way so
that you can always be generous. And when we*

take your gifts to those who need them, they will thank God."

Proverbs 19:4 in the New Living Translation says:

"Wealth makes many 'friends;' poverty drives them all away."

Proverbs 28:27 in the New Living Translation says:

"Whoever gives to the poor will lack nothing, but those who close their eyes to poverty will be cursed."

I could have added many more scriptures to reinforce the seven questions I've asked … but know this, the Bible has an abundance of scriptures to prove the point that God does want you well and financially blessed.

I would, however, like to share one last scripture with you.

Proverbs 20:10 in the Amplified Bible says:

"The blessing of the Lord--it makes [truly] rich, and He [God] adds no sorrow with it [neither does toiling increase it]."

Day 18

How Much of God Do You Want?

I have a question for the men and then for the women.

Men, have you dated a woman or perhaps you're married to *a woman who is only interested in your money and what you could do for her? She wants what she wants when she wants it?*

Have you ever felt that the woman in your life only wants the provision and protection you provide ... *without giving you the affection and intimacy that you so desire?*

Has your marriage relationship or the lack thereof gotten to the point *where she is interested in things other than you ... only focusing on you when there's a need to be met?*

Women, have you ever dated or perhaps you're married to a man who only wants to be seen with you ... because of your beauty and sexual appeal rather than what's in your head or heart?

Have you ever felt like the man in your life focuses

more on his job, golf game, sporting events on TV, buddies, female co-workers than he does on you and meeting your needs?

Does it seem the only time he wants to talk about what's important to you is when he's wanting to satisfy his needs?

Men and women, if you answered yes to any of the questions … **then you can understand how God feels**.

Do we only want to spend time with God when we have a need … financial, physical or otherwise?

Do we only desire His presence when we're broke … *needing money for a payment … or some other sort of financial crisis?*

Do we only desire to spend time with Him *when we've been given a bad report by the doctor for ourselves or someone we love?*

Do we only desire intimacy with Him when facing an adversity, *uncertainty* or seeming tragedy in life?

Can you imagine how God feels?

We need to ask ourselves … What's our relationship with God? Does it parallel that of the children of Israel?

Exodus 20:18-19 in the Amplified Bible says:

"Now all the people perceived the thunderings and the lightnings and the noise of the trumpet and the smoking mountain, and as [they] looked they trembled with fear and fell back and stood afar off. And they said to Moses, You speak to us and we will listen, but let not God speak to us, lest we die."

As I read this passage ... I feel no compassion for the children of Israel. *It's clear they don't have a relationship with God but only want what He could give them. They may have feared Him ... but not in a reverential way.*

Perhaps their relationship is like that of some politicians whose most prevalent thought is, *"What have you done for me lately?"*

When the children of Israel asked Moses *to speak for them* ... they clearly showed they had no interest in direct contact with God ... instead they wanted a mediator. *They were willing to put someone else between them and God which clearly illustrates their lack of desire for any intimacy with Him.*

The children of Israel wanted what God could do for them ... but they didn't want Him. Yet when things weren't going the way they wanted ... the children of Israel became very demanding.

When they complained they were thirsty ... God gave

them water.

When they complained they were hungry … God rained down bread from heaven.

When they murmured about a lack of meat … God caused quail to fall out of the sky.

When they were afraid of their enemies … God gave them the victory.

At every turn … when the children of Israel made a demand … God provided for them and met their needs.

Are we like the children of Israel?

Do we want His prosperity without His presence?

There is nothing wrong with asking God to meet our needs and wants.

In fact, Matthew 6:33 in the New Century Version gives us the divine sequence for prosperity.

> *"Seek first God's kingdom and what God wants.*
> *Then all your other needs will be met as well."*

No question, God is concerned about every need of your life. In fact, God tells us in His Word to ask Him for our daily bread.

Matthew 6:11 says:

"Give us this day our daily bread."

The scripture is clear about God's desire to meet all your needs. But there are two questions which come to mind and must be asked.

How much of God do you want? And why do you want Him?

<u>*Way too many believers treat our Heavenly Father as "iGod."*</u>

If you own and/or are familiar with iPhones, iPads, iPods or any other smart phone or computer that has touchscreen technology, *then you understand this frame of reference.*

On the modern electronic gizmos ... *when you want something, you lightly touch the screen and you've got it.*

Way too many Christians treat God the very same way ... as iGod ... *only touching Him with an iGod kind of experience.*

I googled "iGod" and was disappointed to find that most of the references were ungodly ... and dealing with artificial intelligence.

I felt encouraged when I saw a blog titled, "iGod" ... but the primary thrust of the article was about the writer's love of jazz … and on the side … he expressed love for Jesus too.

The writer mentioned that hearing Ella Fitzgerald sing *All of Me* at the Monterey Jazz Festival kindled his interest in jazz.

When I read "All of Me" … I thought … he's going to discuss giving all of ourselves to God … but he didn't. *However, I feel prompted to share the only part of the song that comes to my mind.*

> ***"All of me, why not take all of me? Can't you see I'm not good without you?"***

Earlier I asked, "How much of God do you want?"

The real question is how much of you does God want? The answer is simple: ***All of you.***

And yes, He wants to bless you … to meet your every need … but He wants you to desire more than anything else to be in His presence.

One more thing … not only does God want all of you … but there will come a day of reckoning.

Amos 3:1 in the New Living Translation says:

> *"Listen to this, Israel. God is calling you to account—and I mean all of you, everyone connected with the family that he delivered out of Egypt. Listen!"*

If God has delivered you out of economic Egypt … the land of not enough … *then your greatest desire should be to make Him more than an iGod* … only there for you to touch when you have a need or a problem.

1 Corinthians 14:4 in the New Living Translation says:

> *"… I want all of you to develop intimacies with God in prayer, but please don't stop with that. Go on and proclaim his clear truth to others. It's more important that everyone have access to the knowledge and love of God …"*

Like I said … He wants more than a touch … He wants all of you.

God loves you for who you are … and that's what He wants as well … we need to love Him for who He is and not just for what He can do for us.

Day 19

Pursue … Don't Follow

I'm going to ask you five questions with the most obvious of answers … but I'm doing so to awaken, provoke and invigorate your thought process. Here are the five questions.

- Do you want to be successful in life?

- Do you want to be prosperous?

- Do you want to be restored to health?

- Do you want to feel alive?

- Do you want to live in God's fullness?

If you answered "yes" to those five questions, then fully embrace the words of Proverbs 21:21:

"He that followeth after righteousness and mercy findeth life, righteousness, and honour."

I felt impressed to look up the word *life* in the *Strong's*

Concordance and it translates to the Hebrew word chay (H2416) which comes from the root word *chayah* (H2421) and it means:

"to live, have life, remain alive, sustain life, live prosperously, live forever, be quickened, be alive, be restored to life or health."

So the key to experiencing the good life … *a life worth living* … is to follow after righteousness and mercy.

In studying this passage of scripture in *Strong's Concordance* I found that many times the words translate exactly how we understand them. *For instance, righteousness means to "live righteous."* No real surprise there.

However, when I look up the word *mercy* I was surprised by the definition. It's the Hebrew word kabowd (H3513) and it means:

"glory, honour, glorious, abundance."

This definition further explains the New International Version translation of Proverbs 21:21 which says:

"He who pursues righteousness and love finds life, prosperity and honor."

Now I want to go a bit further … the King James Version of this verse says that *we're to follow after righteousness and mercy whereas the New International*

Version says that we're to pursue righteousness.

To me *follow* is a more passive word. In fact, dictionary.com defines follow:

"to go or come after; move behind in the same direction."

Whereas, the word *pursue* is defined:

"to follow in order to overtake, capture."

I don't know about you … but I'd rather overtake something than simply follow behind it.

Deuteronomy 28:2 says:

> *"And all these blessings shall come on thee, and overtake thee, if thou shalt hearken unto the voice of the LORD thy God."*

Personalize this verse.

> *"And all these blessings shall come on <<Your Name>>, and overtake <<him/her>>, if <<Your Name>> shalt hearken unto the voice of the LORD thy God."*

When you do what's right before God … *as you pursue Him* … then His blessings will overtake you.

There are a lot of people who have been tithing and

giving offerings *but have not yet seen the manifestation of His goodness, glory and prosperity.*

Imagine that you're walking down a straight, narrow path obeying His instructions ... *but you have not yet experienced His abundant provision in your life.*

As you walk down this narrow path ... **there will be times when you feel all alone *because there is seemingly no one else around*.**

Your journey will sometimes take you through difficult circumstances ... *but you keep pursuing Him and His righteousness.*

The scripture says that the blessings of the Lord will overtake you.

That means you've been out in front of your battle ... *traveling along life's highway* ... feeling all alone ... *but never changing your focus* and/or *your pursuit of our Lord.*

When suddenly ... the sound you hear is the blessings of the Lord coming up behind you as they overtake you.

Are you catching this visual image? *In order for something to overtake you ... it means you must be in front of your deliverance.*

Child of God, there is no equivocation in the New Living Translation of Deuteronomy 28:2:

"You will experience all these blessings if you obey the Lord your God."

Notice this scripture doesn't say that you might, could or should "experience some of these blessings." *No, the verse says that "you will experience ALL of these blessings."*

What are these blessings?

Let's go back to Proverbs 21:21 in the King James Version where we discovered that the Hebrew definition of *life* means:

> **"to live, have life, remain alive, sustain life, live prosperously, live forever, be quickened, be alive, be restored to life or health."**

These are the blessings … ALL of them … that God wants released into your life.

One more thing … **no matter what circumstances, situations or problems come your way … fret nor fear not**.

Psalm 119:143 in the New King James Version says:

> *"Trouble and anguish have overtaken me, Yet Your commandments are my delights."*

Even in the midst of adversity … *you've got to know that God will protect you and that His bless-*

ings will overtake you.

Proverbs 3:25 in the New International Version says:

> *"Have no fear of sudden disaster or of the ruin that overtakes the wicked."*

It's important to realize that you're never traveling alone as you journey toward the debt-free lifestyle … *even though it may appear that way to the natural eye.*

Your Heavenly Father is always on call … ***ready as a first-alert responder to every sinister plot against you.***

Proverbs 3:24-26 in the Amplified Bible says:

> *"When you lie down, you shall not be afraid; yes, you shall lie down, and your sleep shall be sweet. Be not afraid of sudden terror and panic, nor of the stormy blast or the storm and ruin of the wicked when it comes [for you will be guilt-less], For the Lord shall be your confidence, firm and strong, and shall keep your foot from being caught [in a trap or some hidden danger]."*

When you seek the Lord and His righteousness and mercy, He shall be your confidence … which will never become weak but always firm and strong. He will prevent you from being caught unaware of sudden danger, trouble or personal peril.

With your confidence in Him there will be no toss-ing and turning during your sleep because He will make it sweet (Proverbs 3:24).

I am particularly encouraged and strengthened by the Message Bible translation of Proverbs 3:25:26:

> *"No need to panic over alarms or surprises, or predictions that doomsday's just around the cor-ner, Because God will be right there with you; he'll keep you safe and sound."*

There are some political prognosticators of fear that need to fully comprehend the essence of this pas-sage. In fact, I want to say it again.

> *"No need to panic over alarms or surprises, or predictions that doomsday's just around the cor-ner, Because God will be right there with you; he'll keep you safe and sound."*

Proverbs 12:21 in the New King James Version says:

> *"No grave trouble will overtake the righteous ..."*

Trouble will not overtake or overpower you ... but the blessings of the Lord will overtake you when you pursue Him with a passion.

Deuteronomy 28:2 says:

> *"And all these blessings shall come on thee, and overtake thee, if thou shalt hearken unto the*

voice of the LORD thy God."

I don't know about you … but I'm anticipating and expecting to be overtaken by His blessings and supernatural protection … that's why I'm pursuing and not following.

How about you?

4 Things About "Uh-Oh"

Day 20

Uh-oh!

You're in trouble now … *unless* …
well … *okay*, we'll get to that later.

As I was reading the Word … God showed me an *uh-oh scripture*. First, let me correct this commonly misspelled phrase. It's not "ut-oh" but "uh-oh" and according to Wikipedia.com it means:

> **"[Uh-oh is] usually said *in anticipation of something bad about to happen*, with the sly admittance of guilt that one may have caused something bad to happen, *or perceiving that something bad has already happened*."**

With that brief introduction … let's discuss the uh-oh scripture I was referring to.

Jeremiah 17:9-10 in the New Living Translation says:

> *"The human heart is the most deceitful of all things, and desperately wicked. Who really*

knows how bad it is? But I, the Lord, search all hearts and examine secret motives. I give all people their due rewards, according to what their actions deserve."

Let's examine 4 things about the *uh-oh* in these Jeremiah 17 verses.

1.   What's the Condition of Your Heart?

What I've just asked you is *not* a medical question. You don't need a doctor, an EKG or electro-cardiogram to determine the answer to this question.

Jeremiah 17:9 says:

"The human heart is most deceitful of all things and desperately wicked. Who really knows how bad it is?"

What's in your heart when an attractive man or a seductively dressed woman is in your presence? *Are there thoughts lurking in your mind that you think no one else will ever know? If so, you've just made an eternity-changing assumption.*

Job 31:7 in the New Living Translation says:

"If I have strayed from his pathway, or if my heart has lusted for what my eyes have seen, or if I am guilty of any other sin."

You can fool other people about what's in your

heart … but not God.

Job 31:33 in the New Living Translation says:

> *"Have I tried to hide my sins like other people do, concealing my guilt in my heart?"*

Always remember … **God knows what's in your heart. Don't forget … you can't hide from Him**.

Here's the very good news … getting the Word of God in you *is the best heart cleanser* and *problem preventative available to man*.

Psalm 119:11 in the New Living Translation says:

> *"I have hidden your word in my heart, that I might not sin against you."*

2.   I've Got a Secret … Well, Not Really.

Jeremiah 17:10 in the Amplified Bible says:

> *"I the Lord search the mind, I try the heart …"*

As a boy, I remember watching a TV show titled, "I've Got A Secret." The premise was for the panelists to *guess the previously announced secret known only to the moderator and audience*. It was an interesting program which aired from 1952 to 1967.

There is coming a day … *when what's in your mind and heart will be revealed* and *it won't be a*

guessing game or a celebrity television show.

Psalm 44:21 in the New Living Translation says:

"God would surely have known it, for he knows the secrets of every heart."

Uh-oh! Not only will God know the innermost secrets of our hearts ... *but truth be told, our hearts reveal what is living in them and it will eventually speak it.*

Luke 6:45 in the Amplified Bible says:

"The upright (honorable, intrinsically good) man out of the good treasure [stored] in his heart produces what is upright (honorable and intrinsically good), and the evil man out of the evil storehouse brings forth that which is depraved (wicked and intrinsically evil); for out of the abundance (overflow) of the heart his mouth speaks."

Henry Wadsworth Longfellow, considered by many as the most popular American poet in the 19th century, once said:

"A person will worship something, *have no doubt about that.* We may think our tribute is paid in secret in the dark recesses of our hearts, *but it will come out. That which dominates our imaginations and our thoughts will determine our lives,* and our character. Therefore, it behooves us to be careful what we worship, *for what we are worshipping we are becoming."*

3.   You've Got a Reward Coming.

Jeremiah 17:10 in the New Living Translation says:

> *"… I give all people their due rewards, according to what their actions deserve."*

In our contemporary society, *if you tell someone they're going to get a reward … they would assume that it's for something good they've done.*

First, a reward can either be something good or it can be something bad.

2 Samuel 3:39 says:

> *"… the LORD shall reward the doer of evil according to his wickedness."*

2 Timothy 4:14 says:

> *"Alexander the coppersmith did me much evil: the Lord reward him according to his works."*

Second, your reward can be for the good things that you have done.

My favorite scripture is Ephesians 6:8 in the New Living Translation which says:

> *"Remember that the Lord will reward each one*

of us for the good we do ..."

Jeremiah 32:19 in the Contemporary English Version says:

"With great wisdom you make plans, and with your great power you do all the mighty things you planned. Nothing we do is hidden from your eyes, and you reward or punish us as we deserve."

Don't kid yourself ... *everyone will get the kind of reward they deserve for their actions* and their faithfulness to His instructions.

2 Corinthians 11:15 in the Contemporary English Version says:

"So why does it seem strange for Satan's servants to pretend to do what is right? Someday they will get exactly what they deserve."

4.   What You've Sowed ... That's What You Will Reap.

Jeremiah 17:10 in the New Living Translation says:

"I give all people their due rewards, according to what their actions deserve."

Personalize this with your name ... Lana, Nicole, Denise ...

"I give <<Your Name>> <<his/her>> due re-wards, according to what <<his/her>> actions deserve."

In other words … what you sow you will reap.

The last part of Galatians 6:7 in the Amplified Bible says:

"For whatever a man sows, that and that only is what he will reap."

Personalized this … Georgia, Marcus, Rose, Jim …

"For whatever <<Your Name>> sows, that and that only is what <<he/she>> will reap."

If you sow gossip … *you will become the subject of other people's gossip.*

If you sow a negative attitude … *you will reap a harvest of bad attitudes from those closest to you.*

If you sow kindness to strangers … *strangers will be kind to you.*

If you sow financial seeds to bless others … *others will bless you with a harvest of financial blessing.*

The actions that you sow … will be the kind of actions you reap.

Here's a final word … if you want to avoid uh-oh moments in your life … then place your focus on God and His Word.

Your *uh-oh* could be an *Oh, Yeah!*

7 Keys to Success and Victory

Day 21

Every time I read Joshua 1:8-9 … I get fired up.

First, Joshua 1:8 says:

> *"This book of the law shall not depart out of thy mouth; but thou shalt meditate therein day and night, that thou mayest observe to do according to all that is written therein: for then thou shalt make thy way prosperous, and then thou shalt have good success."*

As most of you know … in this verse the words "you" and "your" are found a total of six times. God wants you to be successful … but you've got a part to play.

There are seven powerful keys in Joshua 1:8 … but I'm only going to discuss two of them today … as I want to focus on Joshua 1:9.

First, continually read and study the Word of God.

The King James Version says:

> *"This book of the law shall not depart out of your*

mouth ..."

The New Living Translation says:

"Study this Book of Instruction continually ..."

The Message Bible says:

"And don't for a minute let this Book of The Revelation be out of mind ..."

The Contemporary English Version says:

"Never stop reading the Book of the Law he gave you ..."

No matter what translation you use ... it's clear that we're to be in the Word of God ... not just on Sundays ... *or when times get tough* ... or when there's trouble.

Putting the Word to action *within us* **is a continual process**. It is to be an <u>integral part of our talk and our walk</u>.

Second, speak the Word day and night.

The King James Version says:

"... thou shalt meditate therein day and night ..."

The Hebrew word for *meditate* is hagah (H1897) and it means:

"utter, muse, mutter, meditate, speak."

It comes from a root word that means whisper.

The general impression of the word meditate is that you just think about something *by pondering it in your mind.* However, the Hebrew translation shows that we're not to just ponder and think about the word *but speak it out even in a whisper.*

In Matthew 12:34 in the Amplified Bible says:

> *"… For out of the fullness (the overflow, the superabundance) of the heart the mouth speaks."*

As we continually read and study the Word of God … *we're programming the good stuff (the Word) into our mental hard drives (our brain).*

In the daily situations of life … our response in every circumstance *will be determined by the superabundance of the Word* that's in our hearts and ready to flow out of our mouths.

Now let's move to Joshua 1:9 in the New International Version which says:

> *"Have not I commanded thee? Be strong and of a good courage; be not afraid, neither be thou dismayed: for the LORD thy God is with thee whithersoever thou goest."*

Here are **7 Keys to Success and Victory** in every battle you face:

1. Follow My Instructions.

"Have not I commanded thee? ..."

Psalm 119:60 in the New Living Translation says:

"I will hurry, without delay, to obey your commands."

The Hebrew word for *commanded* means:

"to command, charge, give orders, lay charge, give charge to, order."

You are in a battle against the attacks of the enemy ... in order to repel his attacks you must follow the orders to read, speak and act on the Word of God.

2. Be Strong.

The Hebrew word for *strong* means:

"to strengthen, prevail, harden, be strong, become strong, be courageous, be firm, grow firm."

Ephesians 6:10 says:

"Finally, my brethren, be strong in the Lord, and in the power of his might."

If a boxer wants to win his upcoming Heavyweight Championship fight, he must follow the instructions of a good trainer.

Someone once said:

> *"Invest in yourself. It's like being a boxer; you've got to be in training so when the bell rings, you get your direction, you come out of the corner and you're *ready* ..."*

Your personal trainer (the Holy Spirit) is telling you to strengthen yourself so you can become stronger and *more fit by reading, speaking and acting on the Word of God.*

I'm also blessed by the words of Zachariah 10:12 in the New Living Translation:

> *"By my power I will make my people strong, and by my authority they will go wherever they wish. I, the Lord, have spoken!"*

3. Have courage.

The Hebrew word for *courage* means:

> **"alert, courageous, brave; to exhibit strength."**

The verse says that we're to be strong and courageous. *It's one thing to be strong but it's something entirely different to be "brave."*

Over the years, I've known a lot of people who were

strong but not courageous … meaning **they weren't willing to stand up for what they believe**.

Psalm 31:24 in the New Living Translation says:

> *"So be strong and courageous, all you who put your hope in the Lord!"*

How do you become courageous? The same way you become strong … by **reading, speaking and acting on the Word of God**.

People don't lack strength so much as they *lack the courage to do something* with what they've got.

4. Don't be afraid.

If God tells you to "be not afraid" … how many times does He have to tell you something before you get it and live it?

We are told 26 times in the King James Version of the Bible to *"be not afraid."*

There are 44 verses in the Message Bible that say, *"Don't be afraid,"* and 66 verses in the New Living Translation with the exact same scriptural directive for us.

Regardless of whether you say, *"Be not afraid,"* or, *"Don't be afraid,"* the message is clear … **we have nothing to fear** … because God is on our side (Romans 8:31).

5. Don't be dismayed.

The New Living Translation, the Contemporary English Version and the Message Bible all say, *"… don't be discouraged …"*

Napoleon Hill, self-help author, said:

> "What we do not see, what most of us never suspect of existing, is the silent but irresistible power which comes to the rescue of those who fight on in the face of discouragement."

Deuteronomy 31:8 in the New International Version offers some great advice:

> *"The LORD himself goes before you and will be with you; he will never leave you nor forsake you. Do not be afraid; do not be discouraged."*

Once again, the remedy for discouragement is to read, speak and act on the Word.

6. God is with you.

The Lord your God … your *Jehovah Jireh* (Provider) … your *Jehovah Shammah* (Peace) … your *Jehovah Rapha* (Healer) … He is with you 24/7.

The Contemporary English Version says:

> *"… I will be there to help you …"*

Isaiah 43:1 in the Message Bible says:

"... Don't be afraid, I've redeemed you. I've called your name. You're mine. When you're in over your head, I'll be there with you. When you're in rough waters, you will not go down. When you're between a rock and a hard place, it won't be a dead end— Because I am God, your personal God ..."

Psalm 46:1 says:

"God is our refuge and strength, an ever-present help in trouble."

7. God is with you every step you take.

Joshua 1:9 in the Message Bible says:

"... God, your God, is with you every step you take."

Not only is God with you ... every step of the way ... but <u>He has His eyes upon you</u>. He's watching you. As the popular saying goes: *He's got your back*.

Psalm 32:8 in the Amplified Bible says:

"I [the Lord] will instruct you and teach you in the way you should go; I will counsel you with My eye upon you."

As I read and re-read Joshua 1:8 and 1:9 ... I realize ***just how powerful they are***.

Day 22

Your Trip to Bountiful

Some years ago there was a movie titled *A Trip To Bountiful*.

It was the story of an elderly lady who wanted to visit her hometown of Bountiful, Texas, once more *before she died* … but *her attempts were thwarted by her henpecked son and his bossy wife.*

Just for the record, *Geraldine Paige won a Best Actress Oscar for her portrayal of the elderly lady.*

In the story, she finally "escapes" and begins her trip to Bountiful. I was unable to see the movie but I *heard Cynthia Clawson sing "Softly and Tenderly"* on the soundtrack. It's outstanding.

However, the point of this teaching is not the movie but the title. *It's God's desire that every born-again believer take a trip to Bountiful … not the kind found in a mythical Texas town but in His Word.*

Psalm 119:17 says:

> *"Deal bountifully with thy servant, that I may live, and keep thy word."*

In the Hebrew Concordance of the King James Bible the words *deal bountifully* (ga mail) (gamal) are mentioned 37 times in 32 verses.

The most frequent use (ten times) of the Hebrew word gamal is translated as *"wean" which implies that one form of sustenance is being replaced by another.*

For instance, a child may be weaned from a bottle to a cup and solid foods ... which indicates personal growth and development.

However, in *eight of the 37 mentions in the Hebrew Concordance, the word "wean" is used as "reward."*

For instance, in 2 Samuel 22:21 in the Amplified Bible the word *reward* (gamal) is used as:

> *"The Lord rewarded me according to my uprightness with Him; He compensated and benefited me according to the cleanness of my hands."*

The Message Bible translation of Psalm 119:17 says:

> *"Be generous with me and I'll live a full life; not for a minute will I take my eyes off your road."*

God rewards, *deals bountifully and interacts generously with us so that we "live" according to His Word.*

Consider the *four other times the word bountifully (gamal) is used in the Old Testament.*

Psalm 13:6 says:

> "I will sing unto the LORD, because he hath dealt bountifully with me."

Psalm 116:7 says:

> *"Return unto thy rest, O my soul; for the LORD hath dealt bountifully with thee."*

Psalm 142:7 says:

> *"Bring my soul out of prison, that I may praise thy name: the righteous shall compass me about; for thou shalt deal bountifully with me."*

And, of course, Psalm 119:17 which says:

> *"Deal bountifully with thy servant, that I may live, and keep thy word."*

Now I found it interesting that the word *live* is defined in the *Strong's Concordance* as:

> **"to live, remain alive, sustain life, live prosperously, live forever, be quickened, be restored to life or health."**

With these definitions in mind … I think it's important to re-read Psalm 119:17 again:

> *"Deal bountifully with thy servant, that I may live, and keep thy word."*

God will provide you with sustenance ... He will reward you so you can live ... prosperously ... in health ... to keep (obey) His Word.

Now that's what I call a real Trip to Bountiful ... *the place of God's never-ending generosity and blessings.*

Before I move on ... let me point out that the word bountifully is mentioned one other time in the King James Bible and it is in 2 Corinthians 9:6 which says:

"But this I say, He which soweth sparingly shall reap also sparingly; and he which soweth bountifully shall reap also bountifully."

Enough said ... let's look at Psalm 119:18 in the Amplified Bible which says:

"Open my eyes [to spiritual truth] so that I may behold Wonderful things from Your law."

I have found that when *reading a specific scripture each day for several days, I find different levels of revelation.*

It's like peeling the layers of an onion. *Each layer reveals another ... which brings you closer to the core* ... which in this case is the objective of our search.

I love the progressive revelation of His Word ... my daily prayer is for revelatory insight.

Psalm 119:18 in the New Living Translation says:

"Open my eyes to see the wonderful truths in your instructions."

When the Psalmist says "open my eyes" *it doesn't mean they were shut in the natural.* It simply means *he is asking for a deeper level and clearer revelation to see with his spirit as he has never seen before.*

I'm reminded of when Gehazi, the servant of the prophet Elisha, anxiously reported to his master how their dwelling place was surrounded by enemy soldiers.

2 Kings 6:15-17 in the New Living Translation says:

"When the servant of the man of God rose early and went out, behold, an army with horses and chariots was around the city. Elisha's servant said to him, Alas, my master! What shall we do? [Elisha] answered, Fear not; for those with us are more than those with them. Then Elisha prayed, Lord, I pray You, open his eyes that he may see. And the Lord opened the young man's eyes, and he saw, and behold, the mountain was full of horses and chariots of fire round about Elisha."

Notice in verse 17 the prophet asks God to open Gehazi's eyes so he could see. *The host of heaven had been there all the time but Gehazi's spiritual eyes had to be opened to see them.*

<u>My prayer is for you to open your eyes to the</u>

spiritual truths surrounding you ... the revelation not yet revealed ... the directions not yet received.

You don't need MapQuest for this journey ... you just simply follow His instructions. As you move in obedience to His Word ... *you will see as you've never seen before on your journey to His bountiful provisions.*

Now only that ... but your journey will be successful and prosperous .

Yesterday, I taught Joshua 1:8 and 9 ... this morning I want to share Joshua 1:7 in the New Living Translation with you. It says:

> *"Be strong and very courageous. Be careful to obey all the instructions Moses gave you. Do not deviate from them, turning either to the right or to the left. Then you will be successful in everything you do."*

The instructions from this verse are clear ...

"Be strong and very courageous" no matter what obstacles you must overcome.

However, *being courageous is not enough ... you must obey the instructions you're given.*

When we follow His instructions ... we get His approval. Let me say that again ...

When we follow His instructions … we get His approval.

Psalm 90:17 in the New Living Translation says:

"And may the Lord our God show us his approval and make our efforts successful. Yes, make our efforts successful!"

We're going to see that following His instructions will make you successful and it's profitable.

Now that's a trip worth taking … a scriptural trip to God's Bountiful provision.

Day
23

Be Attractive … Not an Attraction

Have you ever heard the expression that "clothes make the man" ?

Sounds to me like an English tailor coined the phrase … *I know the phrase does have an English origin …* but I can't prove it came from a tailor.

According to most of the sources I googled … *the phrase means that what you wear determines who you are … who you think you are … or who others think you are.*

The assumption is that when you see a person who is well-dressed … it reflects their professionalism and character. *That may have been true in the day … but not in this day.*

I can assure you that a woman with a Versace dress, Louie Vuitton purse, Jimmy Choo shoes and a Christophe hairstyle … *is not necessarily a person of character … truthfully, they're more apt to be a character instead of having one.*

You can be dressed to the nines *but if what you*

say when you open your mouth doesn't impress … it won't matter how you're dressed.

Don't get me wrong … I do believe in dressing for success … *but what I wear doesn't determine who I am.*

There are times when what you wear will get you in a door … *but it will take who you are … to keep you there.*

In 1975, John T. Molloy wrote a powerful little book titled *Dress for Success*. One phrase in that book has stayed with me through the years. He said:

> *"Dress for the job you want, not the job you've got."*

There's a difference in dressing for success … *by busting through your credit limit over designer clothes and accessories.*

I know ministry leaders who will never be seen in anything other than an Armani suit. *If that floats their boat … may they always have wind in their sails.* But that's not me.

I'm not condemning those who choose designer wardrobes … *as long as they can pay for them.*

If you purchase and parade around in knock-off designer clothes and accessories … *the only thing that's fake isn't your wardrobe.*

Are you ready for a good laugh?

Mark Twain said:

"Clothes make the man. Naked people have little or no influence on society."

The inward beauty of our character is more important than outward appearance.

1 Peter 3:3-4 in the New Living Translation says:

"Don't be concerned about the outward beauty of fancy hairstyles, expensive jewelry, or beautiful clothes. You should clothe yourselves instead with the beauty that comes from within, the unfading beauty of a gentle and quiet spirit, which is so precious to God."

Some have used this verse to condemn women for doing things to improve their outward appearance … _that's not the intent nor the heart of the verse. This scripture is about priorities, not judgments._

Our first priority should be inward beauty … the manifestation of the fruit of the Spirit in our lives.

Galatians 5:22-23 in the Amplified Bible says:

"But the fruit of the [Holy] Spirit [the work which His presence within accomplishes] is love, joy (gladness), peace, patience (an even temper, forbearance), kindness, goodness (benevo-

lence), faithfulness, (meekness, humility), self-control (self-restraint, continence). Against such things there is no law [that can bring a charge]."

Manifesting this type of fruit in your life … will produce *"… the unfading beauty of a gentle and quiet spirit, which is so precious to God."*

God is more concerned about what He sees inside you *than what He sees on the outside of you*.

1 Samuel 16:7 in the Amplified Bible says:

"But the Lord said to Samuel, Look not on his appearance or at the height of his stature, for I have rejected him. For the Lord sees not as man sees; for man looks on the outward appearance, but the Lord looks on the heart."

Sadly, we often form an opinion of someone long before they ever open their mouths.

I remember years ago, we frequently used staffing companies to screen potential employees. *They had a code that I found I could take to the bank* … they must have been taught exactly what to say.

If the company told me that a female applicant had a good personality *then I knew her looks were not her strong point* …

If the company said the applicant dressed nicely … *then I knew she had difficulty in keeping trim ...*

Yes, our first impressions are often based on appearance. *I have seen some gorgeous women who were very ugly ... in their heart of hearts.*

One of the best employees I ever hired was vertically challenged. *Meaning ... she was too short ... for the amount of weight she was carrying.* However, she was incredibly efficient.

Truth be told, I don't fit the profile either ... I'm follically challenged ... being almost bald. *I'm in my "mature" years and vertically challenged as well.* Not sure if I'd pass the test in the current job market ... but if an employer needed my skills ... *they would be a fool not to hire me based on what I look like.*

I've even heard people say it doesn't cost any more to hire someone attractive than someone who's ugly.

Truthfully, the attractive person may distract other employees ... *either through lust or jealously.*

The scriptures are very clear ... *keep your priorities right.*

God first. Second, never look to the outward appearance to make a decision ... check the heart first.

The scripture is also teaching that we should judge people based on what they do instead of how they look.

1 Timothy 2:9-10 in the Amplified Bible says:

"Also [I desire] that women should adorn themselves modestly and appropriately and sensibly in seemly apparel, not with [elaborate] hair arrangement or gold or pearls or expensive clothing, but by doing good deeds (deeds in themselves good and for the good and advantage of those contacted by them), as befits women who profess reverential fear for and devotion to God."

Paul is not telling women to ignore jewelry, make-up or flattering hairstyles … but once again … we read where the scripture is stressing priorities.

My philosophy about make-up is simple. If the barn needs painting … paint it.

Here's the bottom line. Someone once said: *"Be attractive but not an attraction."*

Truthfully, women wearing no make-up can make them more of an attraction than wearing some.

I did a teaching titled "7 Ways to Make A Good First Impression." I shared a story about a young woman I interviewed years ago.

This young woman scored *the highest score we had ever recorded on a typing and ten-key test.* It was *off the charts and with no errors.*

The young woman was efficient and very attractive …

but I didn't hire her.

The simple reason is that she was wearing a miniskirt.

I knew that when the other women in that department saw an *attractive woman wearing a miniskirt ... she would never be given a chance to survive. The fresh impression created by her dress would minimize her effectiveness.*

I felt bad about my decision ... talked with my fine wife Bev. We called the young woman back in and explained our decision. We agreed to allow her to come for a second interview and she was dressed much differently.

This woman became one of the most efficient employees we ever had. To this date, she is a *close family friend* who often *counsels women on how they should look when seeking employment. And by the way, she loves God with all her heart.*

However, the way she dressed ... almost cost her a job.

I thought I was through with the teaching ... but I feel impressed to offer a few more Rich Thoughts.

Your priorities are wrong ... if you use your tithes and offerings to buy clothes. Period. Paragraph.

Your tithe and offering money should never be hanging in your closet.

Clothes may influence people but they definitely don't make the man … rather what's inside of you … makes you what and who you are.

Day
24

26 Reasons to Improve Yourself

There are 26 reasons why you should improve your self-image. Here's your A-to-Z list.

A poor self-image ...

Affects Your Attitude

Philippians 2:5 in the New Living Translation says:

> *"You must have the same attitude that Christ Jesus had."*

Blocks Your Blessings

Proverbs 10:22 in the New Heart English Bible says:

> *"The Lord's blessings brings wealth, and He adds no trouble to it."*

Crushes Your Creativity

Galatians 6:4-5 in the Message Bible says:

"Make a careful exploration of who you are and the work you have been given, and then sink yourself into that. Don't be impressed with yourself. Don't compare yourself with others. Each of you must take responsibility for doing the creative best you can with your own life."

Destroys Your Dreams

Joel 2:28 says:

"And it shall come to pass afterward, that I will pour out my spirit upon all flesh; and your sons and your daughters shall prophesy, your old men shall dream dreams, your young men shall see visions."

Energizes Your Enemy

Exodus 23:33 says:

"But if you will indeed listen to and obey His voice … I will be an enemy to your enemies and an adversary to your adversaries."

Fixes Your Finances

Job 42:10 says:

"And the LORD turned the captivity of Job, when he prayed for his friends: also the LORD gave Job twice as much as he had before."

Glitches Your Gifting

Romans 12:6 in The Living Bible says:

"God has given each of us the ability to do certain things well ..."

Handicaps Your Hopes

Isaiah 26:3 in the Amplified Bible says:

"You will guard him and keep him in perfect and constant peace whose mind [both its inclination and its character] is stayed on You, because he commits himself to You, leans on You, and hopes confidently in You."

Ignores Your Ideas

2 Thessalonians 1:11-12 in the Message Bible says:

"Because we know that this extraordinary day is just ahead, we pray for you all the time—pray that our God will make you fit for what he's called you to be, pray that he'll fill your good ideas and acts of faith with his own energy so that it all amounts to something. If your life honors the name of Jesus, he will honor you. Grace is behind and through all of this, our God giving himself freely, the Master, Jesus Christ, giving himself freely."

Jeopardizes Your Job

Ecclesiastes 5:18-20 in the Message Bible says:

"After looking at the way things are on this earth, here's what I've decided is the best way to live: Take care of yourself, have a good time, and make the most of whatever job you have for as long as God gives you life. And that's about it. That's the human lot. Yes, we should make the most of what God gives, both the bounty and the capacity to enjoy it, accepting what's given and delighting in the work. It's God's gift! God deals out joy in the present, the now. It's useless to brood over how long we might live."

Kidnaps Your Knowledge

Proverbs 10:14 in the New King James Version says:

"Wise people store up knowledge, But the mouth of the foolish is near destruction."

Loses Your Leadership

Proverbs 20:28 in the Message Bible says:

"Love and truth form a good leader; sound leadership is founded on loving integrity."

Manhandles Your Motivation

Proverbs 16:10 in the Message Bible says:

"A good leader motivates, doesn't mislead,

doesn't exploit."

Navigates Your Naivety

Proverbs 1:4 in the New American Standard Bible says:

"To give prudence to the naive, To the youth knowledge and discretion."

Obsesses Over Your Obstacles

2 Corinthians 10:4 in the New Living Translation says:

"We destroy every proud obstacle that keeps people from knowing God. We capture their rebellious thoughts and teach them to obey Christ."

Paralyzes your Potential

Ecclesiastes 11:4 in The Living Bible says:

"If you wait for perfect conditions, you'll never get anything done."

Quits your Quest

Proverbs 2:2 in the Amplified Bible says:

"Making your ear attentive to skillful and godly Wisdom and inclining and directing your heart and mind to understanding [applying all your

powers to the quest for it]"

Ruins your Relationships

Galatians 5:14 in the Amplified Bible says:

"For the whole Law [concerning human relationships] is complied with in the one precept, You shall love your neighbor as [you do] yourself."

Sabotages your Success

Jeremiah 29:11 in the New International Reader's Version says:

"'I know the plans I have for you,' announces the Lord. 'I want you to enjoy success. I do not plan to harm you. I will give you hope for the years to come.'"

Targets your Talent

Matthew 25:15 says:

"And unto one he gave five talents, to another two, and to another one; to every man according to his several ability; and straightway took his journey."

Unarms your Uniqueness

Galatians 5:25-26 in the Message Bible says:

"Since this is the kind of life we have chosen, the

life of the Spirit, let us make sure that we do not just hold it as an idea in our heads or a sentiment in our hearts, but work out its implications in every detail of our lives. That means we will not compare ourselves with each other as if one of us were better and another worse. We have far more interesting things to do with our lives. Each of us is an original."

Vacates your Vision

Habakkuk 2:2 in the Contemporary English Version says:

"Then the LORD told me: 'I will give you my message in the form of a vision. Write it clearly enough to be read at a glance.'"

Wastes your Wisdom

James 3:13 in the New Living Translation says:

"If you are wise and understand God's ways, prove it by living an honorable life, doing good works with the humility that comes from wisdom."

'Xcavates your 'Xample

Romans 12:13 says:

"When God's people are in need, be ready to help them. Always be eager to practice hospi-

tality."

Yuks up Yourself

Mark 12:31in the Amplified Bible says:

"The second is like it and is this, You shall love your neighbor as yourself. There is no other commandment greater than these."

Zigzags your Zest

Psalm 27:1 in the Message Bible says:

"Light, space, zest— that's God! So, with him on my side I'm fearless, afraid of no one and nothing."

Here are four more scriptural reasons why you should have a great self-image.

Genesis 1:26 says:

"And God said, <u>Let us make man in our image, after our likeness</u>: and <u>let them have dominion</u> over the fish of the sea, and over the fowl of the air, and over the cattle, and over all the earth, and over every creeping thing that creepeth upon the earth."

Jeremiah 1:5 in the Amplified Bible says:

"<u>Before I formed you in the womb I knew</u> [and]

approved of you [as My chosen instrument], and before you were born I separated and set you apart, consecrating you; [and] I appointed you as a prophet to the nations."

Psalm 139:14 says:

"I will praise thee; for I am fearfully and wonderfully made: marvellous are thy works; and that my soul knoweth right well.

Ephesians 2:10 in the Amplified Bible says:

"For we are God's [own] handiwork (His workmanship), recreated in Christ Jesus, [born anew] that we may do those good works which God predestined (planned beforehand) for us [taking paths which He prepared ahead of time], that we should walk in them [living the good life which He prearranged and made ready for us to live]."

Day 25

7 Things God Will Do for You

Have you ever had someone you could confide in? *Someone you could share your innermost secrets and thoughts with?*

Did this person ever betray your confidence or fail to keep your secret?

Do you realize that you have a friend closer than a brother who will never betray your confidence?

A friend who will confide in you with His innermost secrets?

A friend who will make a covenant with you … guaranteeing your future well-being?

Psalm 25:14 in the New International Version says:

> *"The LORD confides in those who fear him; he makes his covenant known to them."*

The King James Version says:

> *"The secret of the Lord is with them that fear*

him ..."

According to *Strong's Concordance* the Hebrew word for *secret* is cowd (H5475) and it means:

**"council (of familiar conversation);
counsel; intimacy with God."**

Also, according to *Strong's Concordance* the Hebrew word for *fear* is yare (H3372) and it means:

**"to fear, revere; be afraid; to stand in
awe of, be awed; reverence, honour,
respect."**

When you fear and reverence Him ... when you stand in awe of God ... *not only will He confide in you ... establish His covenant with you* ... but there are seven blessings He will release into your life.

1.   He will confide in you ... telling you secrets.

The scripture tells you who you can confide in and who you can't.

Proverbs 20:19 in the Message Bible says:

"Gossips can't keep secrets, so never confide in blabbermouths."

There's an old saying that if you don't have anything nice to say somebody ... then don't say nothing at all.

Truthfully, I prefer the quote by Alice Roosevelt Longworth who said:

"If you haven't got anything nice to say about anybody come sit next to me."

In life there are people you will talk with … *people you will trust and those you won't.*

John 15:15 in the New Living Translation says:

"I no longer call you slaves, because a master doesn't confide in his slaves. Now you are my friends, since I have told you everything the Father told me."

Imagine that … *through our obedience and reverence of our Heavenly Father we can be told everything …* that God told Jesus. Now that's a powerful thought … He will confide in us.

2.   He will be watching over you.

Psalm 33:18 says:

"Behold, the eye of the LORD is upon them that fear him, upon them that hope in his mercy;"

What a joy … *what a comfort in knowing that the Lord has His eyes upon us* … that He is watching over us and protecting us.

Psalm 32:8 says:

> *"I will instruct thee and teach thee in the way which thou shalt go: I will guide thee with mine eye."*

One of my favorite scriptures is Psalm 40:17 in The Living Bible which says:

> *"I am poor and weak, yet the Lord is thinking about me right now!"*

I want you to write down the last part of Psalm 40:17.

> *"… the Lord is thinking about me right now."*

Personalize it.

> *"… the Lord is thinking about <<Name>> right now."*

3. He will dispatch the angels of the Lord to be around you.

Psalm 34:7 says:

> *"The angel of the LORD encampeth round about them that fear him, and delivereth them."*

The Message Bible translation of Psalm 34:7 says:

> *"God's angel sets up a circle of protection around us while we pray."*

His Angels minister to us.

Hebrews 1:14 says:

"Are they [angels] not all ministering spirits, sent forth to minister for them who shall be heirs of salvation?"

In the *Strong's Concordance* ... *ministering* is the Greek word leitourgikos (G3010) and it means:

"relating to the performance of service, employed in ministering."

However, G3010 is from the same root word leitourgeō (G3008) and ... it means:

"to assume an office which must be administered at one's own expense."

Now get ready for the this: the word *ministering* also means:

"to do a service, perform a work of those who aid others with their resources, and relieve their poverty."

As I read the word resources, the Lord brought Ephesians 3:16 in the New Living Translation to my attention:

"I pray that from his glorious, unlimited resources he will empower you with inner strength

through his Spirit."

Angels have unlimited resources in ministering to you.

4.   He will never allow you to live in want.

Psalm 34:9 says:

> *"O fear the LORD, ye his saints: for there is no want to them that fear him."*

I'm also reminded of Judges 18:10:

> *"When ye go, ye shall come unto a people se-cure, and to a large land: for God hath given it into your hands; a place where there is no want of anything that is in the earth."*

Just imagine … *no want of anything.*

Why will you and I never want for anything?

Psalm 23:1 says:

> *"The Lord is my shepherd; I shall not want."*

5.   He will save you.

Psalm 85:9 says:

> *"Surely his salvation is nigh them that fear him; that glory may dwell in our land."*

Your salvation is near you … it's in your mouth.

When you confess your sins, ask for His forgiveness and accept Jesus as the Lord of your life … *reverencing Him … then salvation will be near you …* because God heard your cry.

Psalm 145:19 says:

> *"He will fulfil the desire of them that fear him: he also will hear their cry, and will save them."*

Ezekiel 37:23 says:

> *"Neither shall they defile themselves any more with their idols, nor with their detestable things, nor with any of their transgressions: but I will save them out of all their dwelling places, wherein they have sinned, and will cleanse them: so shall they be my people, and I will be their God."*

6.   He will give you His mercy.

Psalm 103:17 says:

> *"But the mercy of the LORD is from everlasting to everlasting upon them that fear him, and his righteousness unto children's children;"*

According to *Strong's Concordance* the Hebrew word for *mercy* is checed (H2617) and it means:

"goodness, kindness, faithfulness."

The word *mercy* is also *often translated as love.*

The great thing is that His mercy is fresh and new every day.

7.   He's happy with those who fear him.

Psalm 147:11 says:

"The LORD taketh pleasure in them that fear him, in those that hope in his mercy."

Make no mistake about it ... God takes pleasure in you.

Psalm 104:31 in the New Living Translation says:

"May the glory of the Lord continue forever! The Lord takes pleasure in all he has made!"

Not only were you made ... but you were made in His image and likeness.

Genesis 1:26 says:

"And God said, Let us make man in our image, after our likeness: and let them have dominion over the fish of the sea, and over the fowl of the air, and over the cattle, and over all the earth, and over every creeping thing that creepeth up-on the earth."

One final thought ... if you were to ask most people

who they would or could confide in … *I rather doubt our Heavenly Father would be on that list.*

Yet the scripture is clear … **His desire is to talk with you … reveal His secrets with you … and establish an eternal covenant with you**.

Now that's something to shout about.

Day

26

7 Reasons My Reward Is More Than a Trip to Heaven

"He's gone to his eternal reward."

Sounds great, doesn't it? The phrase is *mentally soothing ... emotionally comforting* and *spiritually authoritative.*

The phrase is the religious way of saying that *someone has gone to heaven.*

Nor am I minimizing the ultimate reward we receive as a born-again Child of God ... *the privilege, honor and blessing of being able to spend eternity in His presence.*

However, there are seven reasons why my reward is more than a one-way trip to heaven.

1.   If you give to or do for others ... you will be paid for it ... that's your immediate reward.

Mark 9:41 says:

"For whosoever shall give you a cup of water to drink in my name, because ye belong to Christ, verily I say unto you, he shall not lose his reward."

According to *Strong's Concordance* the Greek word for *reward* is (miss thas) misthos (G3408) and it means:

"dues paid for work, wages, hire."

This is obviously the same kind of wages that an employer would pay an employee for working.

In other words, ***you're on God's payroll because He is going to pay you wages for helping those in need***.

2.   If you do good to your enemies ... you will be paid for it ... that's your immediate reward.

Luke 6:35 says:

"But love ye your enemies, and do good, and lend, hoping for nothing again; and your reward shall be great, and ye shall be the children of the Highest: for he is kind unto the unthankful and to the evil."

Some interpret this scripture as saying *God will only be paying you wages in heaven which prompts a question on my part.*

Why? **Do we need money in heaven?** This is the same Greek word for reward which used in Mark 9:41 and it means "wages."

Have you ever won a trip … where your transportation (air fare) was already paid, your transfers (to the hotel where you will stay) were included, your meals are provided for, your entertainment is included, your room service is without charge, your trips to the spa included and your tips were already covered?

It's all inclusive vacation to paradise … and for that … you don't need wages.

3.   **The Bible also indicates that you will be paid for your good deeds in the resurrection.**

Luke 14:14 in the New Living Translation says:

> *"Then at the resurrection of the righteous, God will reward you for inviting those who could not repay you."*

You're probably thinking … *this verse proves that you'll be paid in heaven for your good works here on earth* … the good things you done … the people you've led to the Lord.

"Yes, Brother Harold, we'll have stars in our crown. That's how God will pay us."

I remember being taught that very thing as a boy …

and for most of my life. *It sounds great … wonderfully spiritual … but it's just not what the Word says.*

The Bible … *might* … loosely imply we will receive a crown. In Revelations 4:4 and again in 4:10, the 24 elders who rule and reign with God are crowned.

The point is … who needs a crown? *We will be living in Paradise with every need fulfilled.* If some Christian feels that a crown will make his or her life complete, *I'm sure God will allow them to be blessed with a crown.*

Our reward is not based on our work … but our faithfulness.

Luke 19:17 in the New Living Translation says:

"And he said unto him, Well, thou good servant: because thou hast been faithful in a very little, have thou authority over ten cities."

4.   When you don't live in fear … you will be paid for it.

Genesis 15:1

"After these things the word of the LORD came unto Abram in a vision, saying, Fear not, Abram: I am thy shield, and thy exceeding great reward."

The Hebrew word for *reward* in this verse and 24 other verses is the word (sa harr) sakar (H7939) and it means:

"hire, wages, reward, pay; fare, fee, passage-money."

Exodus 2:9 says:

"And Pharaoh's daughter said unto her, Take this child away, and nurse it for me, and I will give thee thy wages. And the women took the child, and nursed it."

The word *wages* is the same Hebrew word for *reward*.

Let me share with you two other verses that use the same Hebrew word (sa harr) *sakar*.

2 Chronicles 15:7 in the Amplified Bible says:

"Be strong, therefore, and let not your hands be weak and slack, for your work shall be rewarded."

Ecclesiastes 4:9 says:

"Two are better than one; because they have a good reward for their labour."

5.   When you treat others ... the way He wants you to treat them ... you will be paid.

Matthew 10:41 says:

"He that receiveth a prophet in the name of a prophet shall receive a prophet's reward; and he that receiveth a righteous man in the name of a righteous man shall receive a righteous man's reward."

The word *reward* appears twice in this verse and it's the Greek word (miss thas) misthos (G3408) and once again it means:

"dues paid for wage, wages, hire."

It's the same Greek word also used in Mark 9:41 and Luke 6:35.

6. You will be paid ... for your faith ... just like Abraham.

Romans 4:3-5 says:

"For what saith the scripture? Abraham believed God, and it was counted unto him for righteousness. Now to him that worketh is the reward not reckoned of grace, but of debt. But to him that worketh not, but believeth on him that justifieth the ungodly, his faith is counted for righteousness."

Once again, according to *Strong's Concordance* the Greek word for *reward* in this verse is (miss thas) misthos (G3408). Are we beginning to see a pattern here? As before, the Greek word means:

"dues paid for work, wages, hire."

The Message Bible translation of Romans 4:3-5 says:

> *"For the Scriptures tell us, 'Abraham believed God, and God counted him as righteous because of his faith.' When people work, their wages are not a gift, but something they have earned. But people are counted as righteous, not because of their work, but because of their faith in God who forgives sinners."*

You are rewarded for your work.

1 Corinthians 3:7-9 says:

> *"So then neither is he that planteth any thing, neither he that watereth; but God that giveth the increase. Now he that planteth and he that watereth are one: and every man shall receive his own reward according to his own labour. For we are labourers together with God: ye are God's husbandry, ye are God's building."*

You guessed it ... it's the same Greek word G3408 (miss thas).

Does that sound like the sweet bye-and-bye ... *no, it sounds like now.*

7.   When you do everything as unto the Lord ...

you will be paid.

Colossians 3:23-24 says:

> *"And whatsoever ye do, do it heartily, as to the Lord, and not unto men; Knowing that of the Lord ye shall receive the reward of the inheritance: for ye serve the Lord Christ."*

According to *Strong's Concordance* the Greek word for *reward* is antapodosis (G469) and it means:

"recompence, to reward or repay someone."

The word recompense is used as three different Greek words but all of them are defined as money being paid back.

The Amplified Bible translation of Colossians 3:23-24 says:

> *"Whatever may be your task, work at it heartily (from the soul), as [something done] for the Lord and not for men, Knowing [with all certainty] that it is from the Lord [and not from men] that you will receive the inheritance which is your [real] reward. [The One Whom] you are actually serving [is] the Lord Christ (the Messiah)."*

Final thoughts …

Let me be very clear …

Heaven is the ultimate reward for every born-again believer ... I'm not questioning nor minimizing that glorious truth.

However, I am saying that my reward ... your reward ... is much more than a one-way ticket to heaven.

Our reward is also to be enjoyed right now ... *that's not just my opinion* ... it's the Word of God.

7 Keys to Being Alive and Living in Power

Day

27

1 Corinthians 15:20-22 tells us:

> *"But now is Christ risen from the dead, and become the firstfruits of them that slept. For since by man came death, by man came also the resurrection of the dead. For as in Adam all die, even so in Christ shall all be made alive."*

I felt stirred to look up the words *"… in Christ shall all be made alive"* in the *Strong's Concordance*.

I'm here to tell you … there's a lot more to being alive than not being dead.

Looking up the word "alive" gives us the Greek word zōopoieō (G2227) which opens up a definition that means so much more:

"to cause to live; by spiritual power to arouse and invigorate; to give increase of life; or of seeds quickened into life, i.e. germinating, springing up, growing."

Would it surprise you to know that are *seven keys to being alive in Christ in 1 Corinthians 15:20-22?*

First, He wants you to live.

<u>*There is more to living than just inhaling and exhaling oxygen, occupying space and going through the motions of a daily existence*</u>.

God saved us for a purpose ... that purpose was to look at today *as a day the Lord has made ... not just another day.* A day the Lord has made involves so much more.

He clearly *wants us to anticipate the dawn of a new day with expectancy.* **Greet the day with anticipation and expectation of what He is going to do in and through us** *if we just let Him.*

He does not want us to settle for whatever and whoever comes our way.

The scripture in Luke 19:13 says we're told to *"... occupy until I come."*

I looked up the word, occupy, in the *Strong's Concordance* (G4231 – pragmateuomai) and it means:

> **"to be occupied in anything; to carry on in business" and "to carry on the business of a banker or a trader."**

The word *occupy* also comes from the root of a Greek

word **meaning** *"that which has been done, a deed, an accomplished fact"* or *"what is done or being accomplished."*

As I read these definitions in the concordance, it became even clearer … *our Heavenly Father* does not want us just sitting around *biding our time waiting for Jesus to return.*

God wants us alive and about His business of *occupying* or as the definition indicates … <u>*carrying on business, getting something accomplished wherever we are and whatever we're engaged in doing*</u>.

Second, you've got the Resurrection Power of God flowing through you.

Here are four scriptures which prove … ***you've got the power***.

1.   **Acts 1:8 says:**

"… ye shall receive power, after that the Holy Ghost is come upon you … (then) ye shall become witnesses …"

2.   **Matthew 10:2 says:**

"And when he had called unto him his twelve disciples, he gave them power against unclean spirits, to cast them out, and to heal all manner of sickness and all manner of disease."

3.   Ephesians 3:20 says:

"Now unto him that is able to do exceeding abundantly above all that we ask or think, according to the power that worketh in us."

4.   Romans 15:13 says:

"Now the God of hope fill you with all joy and peace in believing, that ye may abound in hope, through the power of the Holy Ghost."

It's shouting time! *The same Resurrection Power that raised Jesus from the dead … is alive and flowing* in *and through you*.

Third, you need to arouse your faith and expectation every day.

You're alive when your faith is aroused to accomplish more than you ever thought yourself capable of.

When you're faithful to the Lord … you will be alive … forever more.

Deuteronomy 4:4 in the New Living Translation says:

"But all of you who were faithful to the Lord your God are still alive today—every one of you."

Through faith … arouse your expectation … every day.

Psalm 5:3 in the New Living Translation says:

> *"Listen to my voice in the morning, Lord. Each morning I bring my requests to you and wait expectantly."*

Fourth, invigorate yourself … to a life worth living.

As the definition of *alive* says, He wants us aroused and invigorated by His spiritual power working in and through us.

He never wants us to experience rigor mortis of the mind or spirit to where our lives are hardened into a death life or catatonic state.

The word *invigorate* does not appear as a translation in the *King James Version, the New King James Version or the New International Version*. However, you do find it *twice in the Amplified Bible* which by amplification uses all the Greek words available to bring broader meaning to the scripture.

Colossians 1:11 in the Amplified Bible says:

> *"[We pray] that you may be invigorated and strengthened with all power according to the might of His glory, [to exercise] every kind of endurance and patience (perseverance and forbearance) with joy."*

One more scripture.

2 Thessalonians 2:15-17 in the Message Bible says:

"So, friends, take a firm stand, feet on the ground and head high. Keep a tight grip on what you were taught, whether in personal conversation or by our letter. May Jesus himself and God our Father, who reached out in love and surprised you with gifts of unending help and confidence, put a fresh heart in you, invigorate your work, enliven your speech."

Now that's what I'm talking about.

Fifth, increase enriches, enhances and extends your life.

Proverbs 11:24-25 says:

"There is that scattereth, and yet increaseth; and there is that withholdeth more than is meet, but it tendeth to poverty. The liberal soul shall be made fat: and he that watereth shall be watered also himself."

It's interesting to me and certainly worthy of note that *the word **increase** appears in the King James Version of the Bible a total of 147 times.*

By comparison the word ***prayer** is in the King James Version of the Bible a total of 128 times.*

While I'm certainly not minimizing the importance of prayer *at all, I'm simply saying that to minimize the importance of increase would also be a mistake.*

Increase is obviously important to God so it should be important to us as well.

Psalm 115:14 says:

> *"The LORD shall increase you more and more, you and your children."*

Our increase comes through our obedience to His spiritual laws.

Sixth, the seed you sow today ... will bring you a harvest tomorrow.

Your seed is anything you do that helps another. It may be information, encouragement, or even finances. *Whatever it is, your seed is always your door out of trouble.*

Job sowed a prayer of deliverance for his three friends. *Then, God turned Job's captivity around.*

David stopped a tragedy by offering a special offering to the Lord.

2 Samuel 24:25 says:

> *"And David built there an altar unto the LORD, and offered burnt offerings and peace offerings. So the LORD was intreated for the land, and the plague was stayed from Israel."*

Remember this … **_When you let go of what is in your Hand, God will let go of what is in His Hand_**.

Seventh, germinating, springing up, growing … God's plan for your life.

God wants us producing fruit in our lives … manifesting the gifting and blessings of the Lord.

He wants us to greet each new day realizing that we have the opportunity to plant "seeds quickened into life, i.e. germinating, springing up, growing." _God wants us to attempt great things for Him._

In order to have life and experience it more abundantly … we must be ALIVE in Him occupying until He comes again. We must be about His business … which is also the business of living in the world for His glory.

<u>**You can't enjoy the rich and satisfying life He has in mind for us … by just going along … to get along … so you can get by**</u>. That's not what being alive means to your Lord and Savior.

So here's the question … _are you alive with spiritual power invigorating every new day that He gives you?_

If not, what are you going to do about it today?

7 Keys to Entering God's Circle of Blessing

Day 28

Many corporations and network marketing companies call their rewards and recognition program for those who achieve certain goals … the Winner's Circle.

Psalm 25:8-13 in The Living Bible says:

> *"The Lord is good and glad to teach the proper path to all who go astray; he will teach the ways that are right and best to those who humbly turn to him. And when we obey him, every path he guides us on is fragrant with his loving-kindness and his truth. But Lord, my sins! How many they are. Oh, pardon them for the honor of your name. Where is the man who fears the Lord? God will teach him how to choose the best. He shall live within God's circle of blessing, and his children shall inherit the earth."*

You may never make the Winner's Circle but you will always be a part of God's Circle of Blessing.

1.   God is ever ready to instruct and lead you.

2 Timothy 3:16 in the Amplified Bible says:

"Every Scripture is God-breathed (given by His inspiration) and profitable for instruction, for re-proof and conviction of sin, for correction of error and discipline in obedience, [and] for training in righteousness (in holy living, in conformity to God's will in thought, purpose, and action)."

According to *Strong's Concordance* the Greek root word for *profitable* is ophelos (G3786) which means:

"advantage, profit, increase."

The Greek word for profitable is found in two other scriptures.

1 Timothy 4:8 in the New King James Version says:

"For bodily exercise profits a little, but godliness is profitable for all things, having promise of the life that now is and of that which is to come."

Spiritual training will help you now (this life) and in eternity (the life which is to come).

His thoughts and instructions are designed to make you prosper.

2   God will give you His best effort.

Can you possibly imagine anything that would give you a greater advantage *than being the recipient of*

God's best efforts?

Psalm 90:17 in the New Living Translation says:

> *"And may the Lord our God show us his approval and make our efforts successful. Yes, make our efforts successful!"*

Personalize this ... Annie ... John ... Marcie ...

> *"And may the Lord our God show << your name >> his approval and make << your name >>'s efforts successful. Yes, make << your name >>'s efforts successful!"*

When we put Him first ... *when we enter His Circle of Blessing ... then we will receive His best ...* and our efforts will be successful.

2 Peter 1:10 in the Easy-to-Read Bible says:

> *"My brothers and sisters, God called you and chose you to be his. Do your best to live in a way that shows you really are God's called and chosen people. If you do all this, you will never fall."*

3.   God will direct your journey when you allow Him to be your GPS.

Your spiritual GPS is a very powerful tool ... check out these seven features.

- First, your GPS is God's Positioning System.

- Second, your GPS is God's Protection System.

- Third, your GPS is God's Peace System.

- Fourth, your GPS is God's Promotion System.

- Fifth, your GPS is God's Possibility System.

- Sixth, your GPS is God's Power System.

- Seventh, your GPS is God's Prosperity System.

If your destination is being guided by His will ... then you will be blessed in everything your hands find to do.

4. God will pardon the sins of those close to him.

First, let's establish the fact that God forgives sin.

Micah 7:18 in the New Living Translation says:

"Where is another God like you, who pardons the guilt of the remnant, overlooking the sins of his special people? You will not stay angry with your people forever, because you delight in showing unfailing love."

Second, forgiveness of sin comes through your confession.

1 John 1:9 says:

> *"If we confess our sins, he is faithful and just to forgive us our sins, and to cleanse us from all unrighteousness."*

Third, your sins are forgiven according to His word.

Numbers 14:20-21 says:

> *"And the Lord said, I have pardoned according to thy word: But as truly as I live, all the earth shall be filled with the glory of the Lord."*

Fourth, He not only forgives your sins … He forgets them.

Hebrews 8:12 in the New Living Translation says:

> *"And I will forgive their wickedness, and I will never again remember their sins."*

The kind of forgiveness spoken of in these four verses … proves the advantages of being in His Circle of Blessing.

5.   God wants to give secrets to, protect and take pleasure in those who fear Him.

First, God wants to tell you secrets … to confide in you.

Psalm 25:14 says:

"The secret of the Lord is with them that fear him ..."

According to *Strong's Concordance* the Hebrew word for *secret* is cowd (H5475) and it means:

"council (of familiar conversation); counsel; intimacy with God."

Also, according to *Strong's Concordance* the Hebrew word for *fear* is yare (H3372) and it means:

"to fear, revere; be afraid; to stand in awe of, be awed; reverence, honour, respect."

When you fear and reverence Him ... *when you stand in awe of God ... not only will He confide in you ... tell you secrets* ... He will establish His covenant with you.

Second, there will be a circle of protection around those who fear Him.

Psalm 34:7 says:

"The angel of the LORD encampeth round about them that fear him, and delivereth them."

Third, God takes pleasure in those who fear Him.

Psalm 147:11 says:

> *"The LORD taketh pleasure in them that fear him, in those that hope in his mercy."*

Make no mistake about it … *when God takes pleasure in you …* you'll be drawn into His Circle of Blessing.

6.　　God will teach you how to choose the best.

When we give God our best … *He gives us His best.* It's a spiritual quid pro quo or if you want it in scriptural terms … it's Ephesians 6:8 which says:

> *"Knowing that whatsoever good thing any man doeth, the same shall he receive of the Lord, whether he be bond or free."*

I felt prompted to look up *best* at dictionary.com where it is defined as:

> **"Of the highest quality, excellence, or standing; something or someone that is best."**

Without question, our Heavenly Father, in His compassion for us … *gave someone of the "highest quality, excellence and standing" …* He gave His best … *His only begotten Son so that you and I might have life and might have it more abundantly* (John 10:10).

Since God gave His best for us … *should we give any less to Him?*

As I was typing these words, I was led very specifically to Proverbs 3:9:

"Honour the LORD with thy substance, and with the firstfruits of all thine increase."

The New Living Translation of Proverbs 3:9 says:

"Honor the Lord with your wealth and with the best part of everything you produce."

Proverbs 3:8 in the Message Bible says:

"Honor God with everything you own; give him the first and the best."

When we give Him the best ... He will return it to us.

7. God will give you the earth as an inheritance.

Entering into God's Circle of Blessing is not just for our immediate benefit but for the generations to come.

Psalm 25:13 in God's WORD Translation says:

"He will enjoy good things in life, and his descendants will inherit the land."

Let's go a little further.

Isaiah 54:17 says:

"No weapon that is formed against thee shall prosper; and every tongue that shall rise against thee in judgment thou shalt condemn. This is the heritage of the servants of the Lord, and their righteousness is of me, saith the Lord."

According to *Strong's Concordance* the Hebrew word for *heritage* is nachalah (H5159) and it means:

"possession, property, inheritance, heritage."

This Hebrew for heritage appears 222 times in 191 verses in the King James Bible. In 192 times … the Hebrew word is translated as inheritance.

Your heritage as a servant of God is "possessions and property."

When you're in God's Circle of Blessing there is a hedge of protection around you *allowing you to receive the possessions and property that are rightly yours* as a child of God.

Now that ought to make you shout.

Day 29

7 Provisions for the Wilderness Trip

Do you feel like you're going through a dry place?

Does it seem that you're traveling through an economic desert?

Are you ready for supernatural deliverance from your financial wilderness?

If you answered "yes" to any of the previous three questions … **I've got some great news for you**.

Today … *deliverance is coming to your house.* Believe it! Expect it! **Confess It!** *Manifest It!*

Exodus 14:13 in the Amplified Bible says:

> *"Moses told the people, Fear not; stand still (firm, confident, undismayed) and see the salvation of the Lord which He will work for you today. For the Egyptians you have seen today you shall never see again."*

I have taught this passage of scripture on several occasions … *it's so powerful and encouraging.*

The children of Israel were delivered from Egypt by the miracle-working power of God and *He would go on to sustain over three million of them in a desolate and dangerous desert.*

During their forty years in the wilderness … *the children of Israel were rarely in an oasis of comfort.* But yet, during all those years in the Sinai Desert, God provided for His children and protected them from predators … *the two-legged (hostile nations)* and four-legged kind (wild animals.)

The children of Israel survived the wilderness experience because of how God provided for them.

Deuteronomy 29:4-6 in the Contemporary English Version says:

> *"He has even told you, 'For forty years I, the LORD, led you through the desert, but your clothes and your sandals didn't wear out, and I gave you special food. I did these things so you would realize that I am your God.' But the LORD must give you a change of heart before you truly understand what you have seen and heard."*

Here are seven provisions for wilderness travel.

1.   Nobody needed a doctor.

Can you imagine three million people traveling around

the wilderness without ever getting sick?

Deuteronomy 7:15 in the Amplified Bible says:

> *"The LORD will keep you free from every dis-ease. He will not inflict on you the horrible dis-eases you knew in Egypt, but he will inflict them on all who hate you."*

Now the key to the children of Israel being free from disease is found in Deuteronomy 7:16 in the Amplified Bible which says:

> *"You must destroy all the peoples the LORD your God gives over to you. Do not look on them with pity and do not serve their gods, for that will be a snare to you."*

We're not to crave, covet or lust after the things of this world.

2.   Nobody needed shoes.

I remember once owning a pair of Ecco shoes. I wore them almost every day for seven years. Finally, I had to put them aside because the heels were wearing down at an angle.

By any standards, seven years is a long time to wear a single pair of shoes.

But yet, the scripture says the sandals of the children of Israel did not wear out *and you can be assured they wore those shoes seven days a week.*

I'm sure there were a wide variety of sandals among those traveling in the wilderness. Remember, the children of Israel took the valuables of the Egyptians before they left Egypt.

No doubt some of the Egyptians were wearing Jimmy Choo sandals while others came from Cairo Pick-n-Pay. (Laughing) Regardless of the brand and/or cost of the sandals ... none of them wore out.

If you search the scriptures you can find information on a variety of shoes.

Deuteronomy 33:25 says:

> *"Thy shoes shall be iron and brass ..."*

Ezekiel 16:10 in the New Living Translation says:

> *"... and sandals made of fine goatskin leather."*

Regardless of the style of the shoes ... they did not wear out.

3.   Nobody needed new clothes.

For most parents August is clothes-shopping month. The kids are preparing for a return to school and they need new clothes ... *because they've outgrown the ones they wore last year.*

When I was a boy ... if you tore your slacks or blue jeans ... they were patched ... today you buy your jeans with holes already in them.

In my youth, *pants with holes or patches were a sign that you were poor.* Today, pants with holes shows that you have parents who paid way too much money *to buy them that way.*

From grammar school through college we have been buying school clothes because the others wore out or were outgrown.

However, that wasn't the case for the children of Israel. Twice in Deuteronomy we're told that the clothes of the children of Israel never wore out.

Deuteronomy 8:4 in the New Living Translation says:

> *"For all these forty years your clothes didn't wear out, and your feet didn't blister or swell."*

Not only did their clothes never wear out ... neither did their shoes.

Deuteronomy 29:5 in the New Living Translation says:

> *"For forty years I led you through the wilderness, yet your clothes and sandals did not wear out."*

4.   Nobody ate bread but they lived well.

Truthfully, in our contemporary culture we would be

healthier if we curtailed our consumption of bread … especially, bread made with white flour.

In Exodus, Leviticus and Numbers, the children of Israel are specifically instructed to eat bread without yeast during the celebration of Passover. They ate bread without yeast because on the night the death angel passed over … *the bread didn't have time to rise.*

In fact, the scriptures are very specific on how to prepare such bread.

Yet, during the forty years in the wilderness … the children of Israel did not eat any bread.

Deuteronomy 29:6 in the Message Bible says:

"… you lived well without bread …"

No bread … but the children of Israel lived well.

Exodus 16:15 in the Amplified Bible says:

"When the Israelites saw it, they said one to another, Manna [What is it?]. For they did not know what it was. And Moses said to them, This is the bread which the Lord has given you to eat."

5.   Nobody had wine or beer but they didn't lack for something to drink.

Deuteronomy 29:6 in the Amplified Bible says:

"... nor have you drunk wine or strong drink ..."

The Hebrew word for *strong drink* is shekar (H7941) and it means:

"strong drink, intoxicating drink, fermented or intoxicating liquor."

At a time when God was trying to find the heart of His chosen people ... how they would act and react to adversity and opportunity ... He didn't want them living in a buzz.

However, God provided water for the children of Israel throughout their wanderings in the wilderness.

6.   **Nobody would ever doubt who their loving and protecting God was because of what He did for them.**

- God fed them with manna from heaven every day they were in the wilderness.

- God provided water for them out of a rock.

- God protected them from the heat of day and the cold of night.

- God kept their clothing, shoes and tents from wearing out.

- God gave them victory over enemy after enemy.

The children of Israel had to rely on God for everything as they were completely without any measure of support for their survival.

7. Nobody will ever understand what He did for them without a change of heart … but you'd better … if you ever want to reach the Promised Land.

Deuteronomy 29:5-6 in the Contemporary English Version says:

> *"'I did these things so you would realize that I am your God.' But the LORD must give you a change of heart before you truly understand what you have seen and heard."*

Sadly, many people think they're the creators of their own destiny … and while you are … you aren't.

Yes, you must show initiative and yes, *you need to be motivated to achieve success* … however … <u>you will never succeed without His promises, precepts and presence</u>.

When we finally begin to understand, acknowledge, accept and act upon the knowledge that He is the source of our deliverance … then and only then … can we begin our journey to financial freedom … ***and the promised land of His abundance***.

Day 30

7 Ways to Be Truly Happy

Happiness is an outward expression of an inner work ... and it *depends on what you do and how you respond to what happens to you.*

For people to be truly happy ... there must be *an inner realization of the mental and spiritual commitments they've made to be more than what they are* ... do more than what they've already done ... and bless more than they thought imaginable.

Here are seven ways for you to be truly happy.

First—something to believe in

The world is full of unusual people who believe in some really crazy things ... *yet they think they are completely right.*

The people *who think marriage doesn't have to be between a man and a woman actually think they're right.*

The people who think that it's okay *to take the life of an unborn child actually think they're right.*

The Romans who threw Christians into the arenas to be eaten by lions actually thought they were right.

What you think is right … it depends on your moral compass … the belief system you base your decision-making on.

I'd like to think that **when a person's core values minimize or ignore the sanctity of human life … that it's their belief system that is out of whack and not mine**!

Second—<u>someone to believe in</u>

From your earliest memory … you believed (hopefully) that your parents would provide for you. At some age, *some children tragically learned that belief wasn't true*. Unfortunately, some discovered *they could no longer believe in one or both parents.*

Sadly, parents have been let down by their children … even as children have been disappointed by their parents.

During a child's educational experience … *many learn to believe in their teachers because they seem knowledgeable and caring* … at least for the most part.

The students who become athletes learn to believe in their coaches.

We learn to believe our best friend … is someone who will always be there for us.

In a popular culture where people are often mesmer-ized by celebrities who seem bigger than life … *we sadly discover their moral character is smaller than we could have imagined.*

If you're blessed in life … *you'll not be let down too much by your parents, spouse, children, teachers, professors, coaches, best friends, employers* or others in whom you believe. But letdowns happen to every-one … *because nobody has a perfect life.*

However, **there's someone you can believe in … *who will never disappoint you* … let you down or forget about you … *no matter what!***

Proverbs 18:24 says:

> *"A man that hath friends must shew himself friendly: and there is a friend that sticketh closer than a brother."*

Third—<u>something to stand for</u>

Peter Marshall, who was once Chaplain of the United States Senate, said:

> **"… because if we don't stand for something, we shall fall for anything."**

Some people are hesitant to take a stand for their Lord … *for fear of others or what they might say or do.*

If that's you … take heart and be strengthened by the

words of 1 Thessalonians 1:3-4 in the Message Bible:

"It is clear to us, friends, that God not only loves you very much but also has put his hand on you for something special. When the Message we preached came to you, it wasn't just words. Something happened in you. The Holy Spirit put steel in your convictions."

The Holy Spirit will empower you with the courage of your convictions even in the face of seemingly over-whelming odds.

Fourth—<u>something to live for</u>

Joe Louis, the famed heavyweight boxer, said:

"You only live once, but if you do it right, once is enough."

So the question is … *are you doing it right?*

If not, don't be discouraged. *You can get a do-over … with a spiritual make-over.*

Let's go further …

<u>Don't live with a money hangover or live with debt leftovers … get a spiritual make-over which will empower you for a do-over</u>.

So here's the question … what does it mean to live for something?

Surprise … here are seven thoughts.

- **First, discover your core values.**

- **Second, make a commitment to a cause.**

- **Third, be a doer instead of a talker.**

- **Fourth, operate with a plan.**

- **Fifth, put your money where your mouth is.**

- **Sixth, never give up.**

- **Seventh, see the reward … the success … the victory.**

Fifth—<u>something to accomplish</u>

The greatest accomplishment you could ever have is not … being at *the top of your class in high school, college or graduate school … getting the job you wanted with all the perks you prayed for* or *even marrying the person of your dreams.*

The greatest accomplishment any person can ever have … is found in Isaiah 55:11 in the Amplified Bible which says:

> *"So shall My word be that goes forth out of My mouth: it shall not return to Me void [without producing any effect, useless], but it shall accomplish that which I please and purpose, and it*

shall prosper in the thing for which I sent it."

The words you speak … the words that come from the mouth of God … will accomplish everything … it pleases and purposes to do.

One of the most satisfying experiences in the world … is to complete an assignment, achieve a dream and/or do what nobody said could be done.

Sadly, *don't be disappointed if everyone doesn't share your joy, success or your thrill of victory.*

One last thing *… everything you accomplish in this life … is not because of you but Him.*

Isaiah 26:12 in the New Living Translation says:

> *"LORD, you will grant us peace; all we have accomplished is really from you."*

Sixth—<u>someone to partner with</u>

Luke 5:7 says:

> *"And they beckoned unto their partners, which were in the other ship, that they should come and help them. And they came, and filled both the ships, so that they began to sink."*

The word *beckoned* in the Greek means *signaled*. So Peter and his crew signaled their partners in the other ship.

Some scholars believe the partners were people who worked for Simon and his family. I don't believe that to be the case as they would have been called employees not partners. Today maybe … but not back then.

I think it's more probable that James, John and some of the other disciples who had been fishermen were in the other boat. Bear in mind … that *Simon's boat had been used by Jesus to teach the people.*

It stands to reason that the other disciples would have been in a boat as well.

Plus, Luke 5:10 in the New Living Translation says:

"His partners, James and John, the sons of Zebedee, were also amazed. Jesus replied to Simon, 'Don't be afraid! From now on you'll be fishing for people!'"

Truthfully, *who the people in the other boat were … is not as significant as what they were.*

Partners … the root word … which according to *Strong's Concordance* in the Greek means:

"to have i.e. own, possess; external things such as pertain to property or riches or furniture or utensils or goods or food, etc."

<u>*A true partner is someone who will go down the road with you*</u>.

Your partner is there when you're on the highest mountaintop *and when you're traveling through the loneliest valley.*

Seventh—<u>something to hope for</u>

Hebrews 11:1 in the Amplified Bible says:

"Now faith is the assurance (the confirmation, the title deed) of the things [we] hope for, being the proof of things [we] do not see and the conviction of their reality [faith perceiving as real fact what is not revealed to the senses]."

Please notice that the thing "hoped for" is invisible, but faith is the evidence that makes it real. There is no such thing as invisible evidence.

<u>*You can't go into a courtroom and win a case with invisible evidence*</u>. The thing hoped for is invisible.

If you have faith for a new house, the new house might be invisible right now but your faith won't be invisible. <u>If the faith is invisible, the house will never show up either</u>.

The Bible says that our *faith is substance ... or better said ... it is the "raw material" that your financial return will be made out of*.

Hebrews 11:6 says:

"… without faith it is impossible to please him:

for he that cometh to God must believe that he is, and that he is a rewarder of them that diligently (carefully) seek him."

In summing up … **your happiness is dependent on you … and your faith**.

Release to Increase

Day 31

Laws represent absolutes.

The law of gravity is activated when you drop an object and *regardless of its weight* … it falls to the ground.

The law of cause and effect reveals that every action in the universe must be followed by an appropriate re-action *and to this there is no exception of any kind, at any time or for any reason*.

Sir Isaac Newton, in discussing the law of action and reaction, said:

"Every action is followed by an equal reaction."

Whenever we send something out, *it returns in kind to either punish or bless*. That which is sent is the action and *that which returns is the reaction*. Regarding life, *we get out of life what we put into it.*

This is based on the spiritual law of sowing and reaping. What you sow you will reap.

Galatians 6:7 in the Amplified Bible says:

"Do not be deceived and deluded and misled; God will not allow Himself to be sneered at (scorned, disdained, or mocked by mere pretensions or professions, or by His precepts being set aside.) [He inevitably deludes himself who attempts to delude God.] For whatever a man sows, that and that only is what he will reap."

Notice how the Bible says: "What you sow *that and that only* is what you will reap."

There is also the spiritual law of release *which says that you must be willing to release for increase.*

Proverbs 11:24-25 says:

"The is [he] that scattereth, and yet increaseth; and there is [he] that withholdeth more than is meet, but it tendeth to poverty."

Three or four days ago … I pointed out that the word *increase* appears in the King James Version of the Bible a total of 147 times.

I also pointed out that the word *prayer* is in the King James Version of the Bible a total of 128 times.

Once again … I need to point out that while I'm certainly not minimizing the importance of prayer … *I'm simply saying that to minimize the importance of increase would also be a mistake.*

Increase is obviously important to God ... so it should be important to us as well.

God wants us to increase in everything our hands find to do (Matthew 25). *He doesn't want us standing still or just getting by ... He's looking for increase.*

Psalm 115:14 says:

> *"The LORD shall increase you more and more, you and your children."*

Our increase comes through our obedience to His spiritual laws.

So I think it's fair to say that increase is obviously very important to God.

Now let's go a little further.

Proverbs 11:25 says:

> *"The liberal soul shall be made fat: and he that watereth shall be watered himself.*

God makes it clear. *If you scatter your money, it will increase ... and you will be prosperous.* If you hoard too much of it, *more than is proper ...* you will be poor.

The New Living Translation of Proverbs 11:24-25 says:

> *"Give freely and become more wealthy; be*

stingy and lose everything. The generous will prosper; those who refresh others will themselves be refreshed."

Truthfully ... that one scripture says it all.

If you give freely ... *you will become wealthy.*

If you are stingy ... *you will lose everything.*

I thought, "Lord that says it all ... there is no need to go any further." But He directed me to follow His Word.

I found that Psalm 37:21 in the Message Bible offers a little more colorful description of what happens when you are stingy.

"Wicked borrows and never returns; Righteous gives and gives. Generous gets it all in the end; Stingy is cut off at the pass."

I grew up watching western movies and television shows ... *so I understand what it means to say you're "cut off at the pass."* It means you're not going to arrive at your destination *because you've been bushwhacked by the enemy.*

Deuteronomy 15:10 in the Message Bible offers another powerful word:

"Give freely and spontaneously. Don't have a stingy heart. The way you handle matters like

this triggers God, your God's, blessing in every-thing you do, all your work and ventures. There are always going to be poor and needy people among you. So I command you: Always be gen-erous, open purse and hands, give to your neighbors in trouble, your poor and hurting neighbors."

The way you handle your giving … *will determine God's blessings in everything you do.*

Never forget, *regardless of our financial circumstanc-es, God's spiritual laws never change no matter how uncomfortable they make us feel.*

You may be asking, **"Do you mean I have to start giving away my money if I want to be prosperous? That doesn't make any sense."**

You're right. In the eyes of the world, it doesn't make sense because it's viewed as a loss.

God's spiritual laws do not always make worldly sense, *but they are His truths and will always work. Not only do they work but they are absolutes. Giving into the Kingdom is seed* and seed always multiplies into a harvest.

The Message Bible translation of Proverbs 11:24-25 says:

"The world of the generous gets larger and larg-er; the world of the stingy gets smaller and

smaller. The one who blesses others is abundantly blessed; those who help others are helped."

God's spiritual laws will not change. *Release and increase (prosper); retain and decrease (tend to poverty).*

I heard this scripture expressed years ago that when you release what's in your hand, *then God will release what's in His hand.*

No question, **I'd much rather have what's in God's hand than what's in mine.**

Once again, we see the law of release. When we release what's in our hands, then God will bring increase into our lives.

I will always remember where I was standing when a dear friend of our ministry called to say that she was sowing a $21,000 seed into our ministry.

Her oldest daughter was entering college and all she had saved for this event was $21,000 (which wouldn't be nearly enough for even one year) ... *so she decided to release what she had to bring increase into her life.*

Within a short period of time ... *someone she knew well came to her and told her that he felt led to pay for half of her daughter's tuition. Not only that, he was going to pay for half of her other daughter's tuition when she entered college in a year or two.*

When what you have in your hand isn't enough to meet your need … it's time to turn it to seed.

Once again, it's the law of release to increase.

Say it with me …

"When I release what's in my hand, God will bring increase into my life."

It's critically important that you get these teachings down in your spirit.

RichThoughts for Breakfast

Volume 8

Invite Harold Herring to speak at your church, event, or rally.

Would you like to invite Harold to be a guest speaker at your church, event, or rally? Just send an email to:

booking@haroldherring.com

or call 1-800-583-2963

With a mix of humor, practical strategies, and Biblical insight Harold will inspire, encourage, and prepare you to change your financial destiny and set you on the path to not only set you free from debt but keep you free of debt and living the debt free life God has called you to.

Keep Thinking Rich Thoughts,

Harold Herring

RichThoughts for Breakfast

Jump Start Your Day!!

This motivating start to your day is something no one should be without. I guarantee you will be glad you called in.

Harold Herring

712-432-0900
Access Code 832936#

Playback Daily Call

712-432-0990

Access Code 832936#

The call starts at 8:30 AM EST seven days a week.

Practical Strategies, Biblical Insights and Thought-Provoking Humor

These are just a few of the things you are missing if you're not joining us every day for the **RichThoughts for Breakfast** morning call.

Get Ready to be Inspired, Encouraged, and Entertained.

Your Rich Thoughts are your leap to your future success!